TALES FROM THE 1967 RED SOX DUGOUT

TALES FROM THE 1967 RED SOX DUGOUT

A COLLECTION OF THE GREATEST STORIES EVER TOLD FROM THE IMPOSSIBLE DREAM SEASON

RICO PETROCELLI
AND CHAZ SCOGGINS
WITH BILL NOWLIN

SPORTS PUBLISHING

Sports Publishing books may be purchased in bulk at special discounts for sales promotion, corporate gifts, fund-raising, or educational purposes. Special editions can also be created to specifications. For details, contact the Special Sales Department, Sports Publishing, 307 West 36th Street, 11th Floor, New York, NY 10018 or sportspubbooks@skyhorsepublishing.com.

Sports Publishing® is a registered trademark of Skyhorse Publishing, Inc.®, a Delaware corporation.

Visit our website at www.sportspubbooks.com.

10 9 8 7 6 5 4 3 2

Library of Congress Cataloging-in-Publication Data is available on file.

Cover design by Mona Lin
Cover photo: courtesy of the Boston Red Sox

ISBN: 978-1-68358-393-6
Ebook ISBN: 978-1-68358-051-5

Printed in the United States of America

To my wife, Elsie, and my four sons—Michael, Jimmy, Billy, and Danny—the best teammates anybody could ever have while playing the game of life.

CONTENTS

Preface ix

Chapter 1: **THE NIGHTMARE 1963–1966** 1

Chapter 2: **THE IMPOSSIBLE DREAM OF 1967 Spring Training** 35

Chapter 3: **APRIL** 59

Chapter 4: **MAY** 71

Chapter 5: **JUNE** 95

Chapter 6: **JULY** 117

Chapter 7: **AUGUST** 135

Chapter 8: **SEPTEMBER** 169

Chapter 9: **THE DAWN** 199

Impossible Dream: Looking Back More than Half a Century Later 211

Epilogue: After 1967 223

PREFACE

Memories begin to fade over the course of half a century, and sometimes we find ourselves wondering if such-and-such event in our lives really happened, exactly when it happened . . . or was it all just a dream? But if you are close to 60 years old or older and a life-long Red Sox fan, or if you played for the Red Sox back then as I did, you know the "Impossible Dream" season of 1967 was not a dream but a reality that remains vividly etched in our memories for all time.

We can recall exactly where we were and what we were doing when Tony C. hit that two-run homer in the bottom of the 11th to beat the White Sox 2-1 in June; how our hearts stopped on that steamy Friday night in August when Jack Hamilton's fastball crashed into Tony's face, ending his season and shortening his brilliant young career; when we wiped out an 8-0 lead by the Angels two days later and Jerry Adair beat them 9-8 with a stunning home run; and when Elston Howard blocked the plate while right fielder Jose Tartabull—who hadn't thrown out a runner on the bases all year—cut down speedy Ken Berry for a game-ending double play as we held on to beat the White Sox 4-3 in a crucial game later that month.

Maybe you were even among the 15,000 insane fans who overran Logan Airport and welcomed us home the night we returned from a road trip riding the crest of a 10-game winning streak. For the last 50 years I have clearly seen Rich Rollins' pop-up descending into my glove for the final out as we clinched our first pennant in 21 years and only second for the Red Sox in almost half a century at the Fenway madhouse on the final day of the 1967 season, and I will clearly see the rotating red seams of that baseball floating down from the heavens for the rest of my life. If you were there, watching on TV, or listening on the radio, I know you'll never forget that moment either.

Before that all happened during that wild, crazy, and unforgettable summer of 1967, the notion of the Red Sox winning the pennant was truly an "Impossible Dream." The odds of us winning the pennant were 100-to-1. The Red Sox hadn't had a winning season in eight years. We had lost 100 games two years before, and in 1966 we had finished ninth, 26 games behind the Orioles and a half-game out of the cellar. We were a very young team, and by the time the season was over we had earned the moniker "The Cardiac Kids" because of our repeated incarnations as baseball's Lazarus. We spent exactly six days in sole possession of first place the entire season, and our largest lead was 1 ½ games. It was a taut four-team race between us, Minnesota, Detroit, and Chicago until the final few days. We had to sweep a two-game series from the Twins to win the pennant, and, while Tom Yawkey was the nominal owner of the club, it was the Twins who figuratively owned us. They had clobbered us 17 times in 18 games when they won the pennant in 1965, and heading into the final weekend of 1967 we were 17–53 against them over four seasons. Who in their right minds would have dared to imagine we could beat a veteran team like Minnesota even once, much less twice, with the pennant on the line?

The average age of our regular lineup in 1967 was 23 ½. We were today's Mookie Betts, Xander Bogaerts, and Jackie Bradley Jr. Carl Yastrzemski was our "old man," our David Ortiz, winning the Triple Crown by hitting .326 with 44 homers and 121 RBIs while delivering clutch hit after clutch hit . . . and he was only 28 years old!

Now "The Cardiac Kids" are getting along in years and these days worry about cardiac arrest instead of hitting 3-and-2 curveballs at the knees with the bases loaded and two outs in the bottom of the ninth. We have already lost many of our teammates: Tony Conigliaro, George Scott, Joe Foy, Jerry Adair, John Wyatt, Elston Howard, Russ Gibson, Bob Tillman, Norm Siebern, Dennis Bennett, Jerry Stephenson, Ken Brett, Dan Osinski, Don McMahon, and our irascible manager Dick Williams. But they are not forgotten and live on in our memories forever.

And here's something else to remember and never forget: The 1967 "Impossible Dream" Red Sox saved baseball in Boston. Without us there would be no Fenway Park with its record streak of sellouts and almost certainly no Red Sox to bring three World Series titles and 50 more years of excitement to Boston and New England.

As late as June in 1967 Mr. Yawkey was talking seriously about either selling the Red Sox or moving the team out of Boston if the city or state did not come up with the money to build a new ballpark, and few people seemed to care if we left. Attendance had been plummeting for years. We had drawn only 811,000 fans in 1966, and the club had not drawn a million since Ted Williams hit that home run in his final at-bat in 1960. I can remember some games when there were only a few hundred people scattered throughout the stands . . . and they weren't very nice to us.

But by the end of the "Impossible Dream" season 1,727,832 fans had packed themselves into aging Fenway Park, setting a Red Sox attendance record. Over the next 50 years the Red Sox never played before fewer than a million fans at Fenway and have routinely drawn between two million and three million fans every year. Without 1967, that might never have been possible.

Oh, had the "Impossible Dream" never happened and Mr. Yawkey made good on his promise to pull the Red Sox out of Boston, no doubt someone eventually would have brought a major-league franchise back to the city. There is too much tradition in Boston for the city to have gone without baseball for very long. But it would not have been the same. It's not likely we would have seen many or even any of the great Red Sox players who came later like Jim Rice, Fred Lynn, Carlton Fisk, Luis Tiant, Wade Boggs, Roger Clemens, Dwight Evans, Nomar Garciaparra, Pedro Martinez, Manny Ramirez, David Ortiz, or Dustin Pedroia.

The 1967 Red Sox forged an unbreakable bond with our fans that continues to this very day. We gave them the most unexpected of gifts that summer—the pennant—and in return they have given us the gift of unconditional love. I have said it before, and I will say it again: No idols could receive more reverence, more appreciation, more gratitude, than the members of the "Impossible Dream" team have received from Red Sox fans over the last half century, especially those of us who made New England our home after our playing careers had ended. To have made so many people so happy is the greatest reward of all. Fifty years and two generations of Red Sox fans later, we are still recognized everywhere we go, and every long-time fan we meet has a personal tale to tell us about how much the summer of '67 meant to him or her.

And now have I got some tales to tell you . . .

1

THE NIGHTMARE

1963–1966

"We were the Mets before there were the Mets."

—Carl Yastrzemski

1963

You cannot truly appreciate the euphoria of a dream unless you've experienced the horrors of a nightmare. For the Boston Red Sox, the nightmare began in the late 1950s. The exciting and talented clubs of the late 1940s, which included the 1946 squad that won 104 games and the AL pennant, and the 1948 and 1949 teams that came within a whisker of winning the flag again, were by then long gone. Bobby Doerr, Dominic DiMaggio, Johnny Pesky, Vern Stephens, Mel Parnell, and so many other Red Sox stars had retired. The incomparable Ted Williams was still playing, and in the twilight years of his career, he was still a better hitter than most players in their prime could ever dream of being. The Red Sox had a handful of other good players—such as Gold Glove third baseman Frank Malzone and right fielder Jackie Jensen, who was the league's MVP in 1958—but there weren't nearly enough of them.

In 1959, the Red Sox finished in fifth place with a 75–79 record, 19 games behind the AL champion Chicago White Sox; and things would get worse over the next seven years. When Williams retired after the 1960 season, attendance at Fenway Park dropped below a million and stayed there for six years. By 1965, when the Red Sox lost 100 games and sometimes drew fewer than 1,000 fans to their games, Tom Yawkey was so discouraged that he talked about selling the team or, even more unthinkable, moving it to another city.

Nobody cared about the Red Sox. In 1965, a lot of the players lived in a huge apartment complex in Peabody, north of Boston. We were pariahs. No one bothered us. No one wanted our autographs. The newspapers dubbed us the "Jersey Street Jesters." (Yawkey Way was named Jersey Street in those days.)

I followed the other professional sports teams in Boston, but it was always difficult to determine where the fans placed their passion. The Bruins were just as bad as the Red Sox were in those years. The Bruins hadn't had a winning season or made the Stanley Cup playoffs since 1958, the last time the Red Sox had a winning record. The Bruins had eight straight losing years that coincided with the Red Sox' string of losing seasons, and the Bruins finished last six times in those eight years, which we never did. But every time the Bruins played at Boston Garden, they played in front of a packed house of 13,909. We were the Jersey Street Jesters, but nobody was calling the Bruins the "Causeway Street Clowns." Fenway had 33,000 seats, and we were lucky if we drew 33,000 fans during a 10-game homestand. Not until Bobby Orr arrived in 1966 did the fortunes of the Bruins start to change—and they became even more popular, if that was possible.

The Boston Patriots, who played their inaugural game in 1960, were pretty good. They usually won more than they lost, made the playoffs twice while the Red Sox and Bruins were losing all those games, and won a division title in 1963. But they didn't draw all that well. The Patriots didn't have a permanent

I was only 20 years old when I made my debut with the Boston Red Sox in September 1963. (*Courtesy of the Boston Red Sox*)

home—they even played their home games at Fenway Park for a while—and a lot of football fans didn't take the American Football League seriously. Most football fans in New England followed the New York Giants and saw no reason to switch their allegiance to a team in an outlaw league.

The Boston Celtics, however, were great. Led by Bill Russell and Bob Cousy and their coach, Red Auerbach, the Celtics won eight consecutive NBA titles from 1958–65. But the public either didn't care or took them for granted. Most nights, the Celtics were lucky to fill half the Garden. Boston sports fans would rather watch the Bruins lose than the Celtics or Patriots win, and they didn't want to watch the Red Sox at all.

AN INVITATION TO THE COUNTRY CLUB

I arrived in Boston for the first time in September of 1963. I was 20 years old, and it was an eye-opening experience for me. I had played only two years in the minors and had hit .239 with 19 homers and 78 runs batted in at Class AA Reading during the 1963 season. But I had made the Eastern League's All-Star team, and the Red Sox brought me up for the final month of the season just so I could get a feel for the major leagues. I got to meet the players and observe a lot. I knew I wasn't going to play much, even though the Red Sox were already doomed to another losing season.

I was aware of the Red Sox' reputation before I got to Boston. Everyone in baseball called them a "country club" team, the "Gold Sox." There seemed to be no pressure to win, and they were well compensated for not winning. Mr. Yawkey was a generous guy. Whitey Ford, who pitched for all those great New York Yankees teams in the late '50s and early '60s, said that the Yankees players all envied the Red Sox, who earned more than they did. Ford said that every time one of the Yankees asked for a raise, he'd be told that cashing his check from his winning share of the World Series in October would be his raise.

Coming up through the minors, I had heard the stories about the Boston country club. But I didn't know if what I heard were tall tales or the truth until I got there in September of 1963.

It was the truth.

THE FIRST WORKOUT

I had already gotten a glimpse of what sort of team the Red Sox were in spring training that year in Scottsdale, Arizona. It was my first big-league camp. There were a lot of veteran guys on the team—a lot of older guys from other organizations, like Dick Stuart, Eddie Bressoud, Roman Mejias, and Felix Mantilla. Dick Williams, a utility infielder who was nearing the end of his playing career, was there, too. Already he had that sneer, like a guy standing on a street corner looking for a fight, which would become so familiar to us when he managed us in 1967. At 23, Carl Yastrzemski might have been the youngest veteran guy there.

Anyway, I was 19 years old, an impressionable kid, and the first day I got to camp, the pitchers lined up for wind sprints. They ran one sprint, and they all fell down, gasping for breath. They were even throwing up right there on the field! I said to myself: "What the hell is going on here? One stinking wind sprint?"

They were all hung over from drinking the night before. But that was spring training.

MEETING DOCTOR STRANGEGLOVE

Now it was September, and I was in Boston with the big club again. Our first baseman, Dick Stuart—Dr. Strangeglove—was battling for the home run title with Minnesota's Harmon Killebrew. Near the end of the season, we played the Twins at Fenway. Stuart had 41 homers and Killebrew 40, and I was going to be playing my first major-league game in the first game of a doubleheader. I was sitting on the bench before the game, next to Stuart, and he said to me: "They don't like me."

"Who? Who doesn't like you?" I asked.

"Our pitchers," he said. "They don't like me because I can't catch the ball. You watch. They're going to throw the ball right down the middle to Killebrew. They don't want me to win the title."

I couldn't decide whether he was kidding or crazy.

It was the first game of the series, the first inning. Killebrew came up against Bill Monbouquette, who had already won 20 games, and . . . *bang*! Stuart came into the dugout after the inning and said to me: "What'd I tell you? Right down the middle! They're throwing 'em right down the middle!"

Killebrew hit another homer off Monbo in the fifth, his 42nd, putting him ahead of Stuart. Big Stu responded by hitting one in the sixth off Lee Stange, and they were tied again.

In the eighth inning, we were still in the game, only down three runs, 7–4; but the Twins started to put together a big inning. A couple more runs scored, and I had a chance to end it before Killebrew got up again when I got a double-play ball hit right at me. But I booted the thing for an error. Stuart looked at me, and I looked at him, and I said: "Honest, Dick! I swear I didn't do it on purpose!" Well, Killebrew came up and hit his third homer of the game, a three-run blast off Arnold Earley that made the score 13–4.

After the game, Stuart said to me, "You, too?"

"Dick," I said, "I barely know you!"

Killebrew hit another one in the second game of the doubleheader off Gene Conley, and one more the next day off Bob Heffner. And that's the way the home run race ended, Killebrew hitting 45 and Stuart 42.

I find it hard to believe that the Red Sox pitchers were grooving balls to Killebrew. But Stuart certainly believed they were, although he was a little more diplomatic with the press than he had been with me in the dugout. He told the newspapermen: "Hell,

Dick Stuart (left) and Willie Mays were two of baseball's premier sluggers in the early 1960s. (*Courtesy of the Boston Red Sox*)

Killebrew had a distinct advantage. If I could have hit against our pitching staff, I'd have hit ten."

Bill Monbouquette says the Red Sox pitchers actually liked Stuart personally. He was fun to be around, and it wasn't that he didn't try or didn't care when he was in the field. He just couldn't play defense, and, of course, this was 10 years before the introduction of the designated hitter. Monbo remembers getting ready to deliver a pitch one time when a roar unexpectedly went up from the crowd. He stepped off the rubber to look around and see what the excitement was all about, and Stuart had just picked up a hot dog wrapper that had blown onto the field and was getting a standing ovation from the fans.

The exception among the pitchers was Earl Wilson. He hated Dick Stuart. One day, when Wilson was pitching, somebody hit a pop fly to the first-base side of the mound. Everybody knew Stuart wasn't going to catch it, so Frank Malzone raced over from third base; Eddie Bressoud dashed over from shortstop; and they collided and fell down. The ball landed untouched at Stuart's feet, and he calmly reached down, picked it up, and handed it to Wilson. Everybody in the dugout was laughing hysterically, but Wilson was in a rage. Monbo said, "Somebody had better go out there and calm him down before he kills Stuart."

GOOD STATS, BAD RECORD

The Red Sox finished the 1963 season in seventh place with a 76–85 record, 28 games behind the Yankees. Yaz won his first batting crown, hitting .321, and also led the league in hits with 183 and doubles with 40. While Stuart didn't win the home-run crown, he did lead the league with 118 RBIs. He also led the league's first basemen in errors with 29. Bressoud hit 20 homers, and outfielder Lu Clinton belted 22. Monbouquette ended the year with a 20–10 record, and Dick Radatz had a great year out of the bullpen, finishing second in the league with 25 saves while posting a 15–6 record with a 1.97 ERA and fanning 162 batters in 132 innings. Yet, only the last-place Washington Senators gave up more runs than the Red Sox.

1964

I didn't go back to Boston in 1964. I spent the entire season playing for Seattle in the Class AAA Pacific Coast League. I was still only 20 years old when the season began, and I was in way over my head. The pitchers in that league had moving fastballs and sliders like I'd never seen before. I hit only .231 with 10 homers and 48 RBIs in 134 games, and for the first time in my brief professional career, I didn't make the league's All-Star Team. I adjusted to the fielding faster than I did to the pitching. The hitters in the big leagues hit the ball harder than the Triple-A hitters. Fielding was just basic stuff to me.

The Red Sox weren't concerned that I didn't hit as well as I would have wanted. I knew they were rushing guys through the organization, and I was one of those guys. Looking back, I probably could have benefited from spending a couple more years in the minors. I really finished my development in the big leagues.

Johnny Pesky was managing the Red Sox then, and he knew the club would never contend with the fading, one-dimensional

Red Sox general manager Mike Higgins (left) and field manager Johnny Pesky were all smiles here. But Higgins wouldn't let Pesky keep the younger players he wanted, and Higgins fired him after less than two seasons. (*Courtesy of the Boston Red Sox*)

veteran players he had in 1963. He lobbied to bring up a lot of the organization's young prospects in 1964, figuring he'd rather lose with players who had a future than with players who didn't. Neil Mahoney, who ran the farm system, agreed with him. "Bring up the kids! What have we got to lose? At least there will be some excitement!" Mahoney said, or so we heard through the grapevine.

But Mike Higgins, the general manager, wouldn't let Pesky keep the kids. Higgins felt more comfortable with veteran players. We all knew that. Pesky had to fight tooth and nail just to convince Higgins to let him bring Tony Conigliaro north with the big club.

TONY C.

Tony C. was even younger than I was, just 19, and while I was already playing in Double-A at his age, he had played only one year of pro ball, and it was in Class D, the lowest level in the minor leagues.

Tony had been born in Revere, just a few miles from Fenway Park, and grown up in Swampscott, a town just north of Boston. He was a terrific all-around athlete at St. Mary's High School in Lynn, and he had baseball superstar written all over him. The Red Sox signed him on September 10, 1962, and sent him to Wellsville, New York, in the New York-Penn League the following spring. The minor leagues had just undergone a major restructuring during the winter, and the NY-PL had been reclassified as an A league, but it was still the bottom rung of the minor-league ladder. You could dress it up as an A league, but everyone knew the baseball was only D caliber.

Conigliaro tore up the league. He hit .363 with a league-leading 42 doubles, 24 homers, 74 RBIs, and a .730 slugging percentage in just 83 games. If he hadn't missed the start of the season—his uncle broke his thumb while throwing batting practice to him that spring—he might have led the league in everything. Naturally, he was a cinch for the All-Star Team. George "Boomer" Scott was also on that Wellsville club, playing third base, and he made the All-Star Team, too, by hitting .293 with 15 homers and 74 RBIs in 106 games.

The Red Sox invited Tony C. to spring training in 1964, and he put on such a good show that Pesky kept him over Higgins' wishes. Conigliaro more than justified Pesky's confidence in him that year. He hit a home run in his first at-bat at Fenway Park and finished his rookie year at .290 with 24 homers, 21 doubles, and

Red Sox general manager Dick O'Connell (center) gets two Conigliaro brothers under contract, Billy (left) and Tony. In 1970, Billy and Tony would play together in the Red Sox outfield and combine for 54 home runs. (*Courtesy of the Boston Red Sox*)

52 RBIs in 111 games. His numbers would have been even more impressive had he not missed several weeks with a couple of broken bones. Baltimore's Moe Drabowsky broke his wrist with a pitch on May 6, and 11 weeks later Cleveland's Pedro Ramos hit him with a pitch and fractured his forearm. Incredibly, Tony didn't get a single vote for Rookie of the Year. Minnesota's Tony Oliva, who won the batting title with a .323 average, received 19 of the 20 votes cast by members of the Baseball Writers Association of America, and Wally Bunker, who won 19 games for the Orioles, got the other vote.

The only other kid Higgins let Pesky keep was 21-year-old second baseman Dalton Jones, who became my roommate when I finally arrived in Boston for good the following year.

A FALSE START

It looked like Higgins had been right to keep the veterans when the Red Sox got off to an unexpectedly strong start in 1964. A five-game winning streak and eight wins in nine games gave them a 20–18 record, and they were only four games out of first place on May 26.

They were still over .500 as late as June 17, trailing the Orioles by only six games. Five wins in six games got them back to .500 at 52–52 on the last day of July, rekindling hopes they might be primed to make a run for the pennant.

Then the Red Sox fell apart.

Seven straight losses and 12 defeats in 13 games knocked them right out of the race. Losing eight of nine at the end of August dropped them into eighth place, 21 games behind. Pesky was fired with two games left in the season and replaced by coach Billy Herman, who thought more like Higgins.

The Red Sox finished eighth with a 72–90 record, 27 games behind the Yankees. Individually, some guys had very good seasons.

Dick Stuart was second in the league in RBIs with 114 and hit 33 homers, but he also led first basemen in errors with 24. Felix Mantilla came out of nowhere to hit 30 homers, and Eddie Bressoud, the shortstop, was second in the league with 41 doubles while hitting .293 with 15 homers. Dick Radatz was overpowering again, leading the pitching staff with 16 wins while also leading the league with 29 saves and posting a 2.29 ERA. Radatz also set a major-league record for relievers by striking out 181 batters in 157 innings, a record that still stands.

The Red Sox hit a franchise-record 186 homers, but the bottom line was that they still gave up more runs than any team in the league except Kansas City.

Carl Yastrzemski had slipped a bit after winning the batting title in 1963. But Yaz and Tony C. were the kind of talents a team could build around, if only the Red Sox were patient enough to do it. With Higgins and Herman running the show, it didn't seem things were likely to change in 1965.

But they did.

1965

I don't know who got Tom Yawkey's ear in 1965. Maybe it was Neil Mahoney, the farm director. Or maybe it was Dick O'Connell, a guy who had never played pro ball, but whose influence and prestige were growing since he'd spent 20 years with the organization. Whoever it was, Mr. Yawkey was prodded into changing the status quo after six straight losing seasons. The change was gradual at first, and general manager Mike Higgins and manager Billy Herman weren't happy about it.

Tony Conigliaro had come up in 1964 after just one year in the minors, against the wishes of Higgins, and had a terrific rookie year. Now it was my turn to break into the lineup, even though I wasn't really ready yet. The Red Sox also kept 23-year-old Jim

Lonborg, who had no more business being in the big leagues than I did, and thrust him right into the rotation.

Lonnie was a very bright guy, a Stanford grad with a degree in biology. (He would become a dentist after his baseball career was over.) Yet, he had pitched only 31 games and fewer than 200 innings in the minors before sticking with the Red Sox. Lonnie and I had played together in Seattle the previous year, and he hadn't exactly dazzled Pacific Coast League hitters, going 5–7 with a 4.84 ERA.

I knew right away that Herman, like Higgins, felt a lot more comfortable surrounded by veteran players than kids. He had

Billy Herman didn't have much faith in young players and let the veterans set their own rules when he managed the team in 1965-66. *(Courtesy of the Boston Red Sox)*

trouble with young kids. He didn't have a lot of patience. Not that Dick Williams did, either, when he took over as manager in 1967, but at least he let the kids play. Herman only wanted to play the veterans. He also detested Carl Yastrzemski. He wanted to trade both Yaz and Tony C., but he was stuck with them. Certainly some of the things Yaz did in those days irked people. For example, if a ball was hit down the left-field line, and Yaz knew it was a sure double, he'd lope after the ball. Some people would get ticked off when he did that. He'd also refuse to chase after obvious home-run balls. Sometimes, he'd just bow his head and put his hands on his knees. The pitchers weren't thrilled with that. Yaz was only 25 in 1965, still a kid in a lot of ways even though it was his fifth year in the big leagues. But even when he was still playing left field and winning Gold Gloves in his late 30s, he wouldn't make a show of chasing a home run he knew was going to end up on the other side of Lansdowne Street.

MANAGING THE COUNTRY CLUB

One thing that wasn't changing yet was the Red Sox' reputation as a country club. Billy Herman did nothing to dispel that image.

"I don't care if a player of mine has a drink. In fact, if I meet one of my players in a bar, I'll buy him a drink," he said during spring training.

When asked if he planned to institute a curfew, Herman replied: "I'll let the players decide themselves if they'll have a curfew this year."

Herman always remembered to take his golf clubs with him on road trips.

A CHANGING CAST OF CHARACTERS

Oh, one thing had changed. Higgins had traded Dr. Strangeglove, Dick Stuart, and his 75 home runs, 232 RBIs, and 53 errors in two

Red Sox seasons to the Philadelphia Phillies for pitcher Dennis Bennett. Bennett, however, was just as much of a character as Stuart was. Whereas Stuart was frightening on the field, with both his bat and glove, Bennett was frightening off it.

One night during spring training in Arizona, Bennett decided to stage his own personal gunfight at the O.K. Corral—with himself. He walked out the front door of his motel room in Scottsdale with a couple of pistols and started firing them. Earl Wilson was rooming nearby, heard the shots, and turned white. Wilson, by the way, was black.

"I had these pistols, and it was Arizona; so, why not?" Bennett explained.

Bennett wasn't really a bad guy, but he never thought the rules applied to him, which made him a perfect fit in Boston, where there were no rules.

When he threw his first complete game for the Red Sox after having undergone arm surgery in Philadelphia, he tossed a champagne party and invited the writers. In 1967, after he pitched a shutout in Anaheim, the writers reciprocated by throwing a party for Bennett at the Playboy Club in Los Angeles. The writers liked Bennett because, as they say, he was good copy.

One day in Washington, he gave up a 480-foot home run to Frank Howard. That night, he missed curfew. When he finally wandered into the hotel, Billy Herman asked where he'd been. "At the ballpark, watching them paint the seat that Howard hit," Bennett explained.

Another time, he missed a team flight from Anaheim to Minneapolis. The Red Sox were taking batting practice the next evening at Metropolitan Stadium, and there was still no sign of Bennett.

"If he's not here by 6:15," Herman fumed, "he's fined $500."

At 6:12, Bennett strolled casually onto the field.

"What's all the fuss?" he asked innocently.

Pitcher Dennis Bennett blended in perfectly with the Country Club Red Sox teams of the early 1960s. (*Courtesy of the Boston Red Sox*)

PLAYING MORE THAN JUST BASEBALL

Toward the end of spring training, the Red Sox began barnstorming their way east. We had a couple of exhibition games scheduled against the Chicago Cubs, and where do you imagine those games were played? Las Vegas, Nevada! I don't know who came up with that brilliant idea.

The ballpark in Vegas didn't have much in the way of amenities, so we had to change into our uniforms in the hotel before taking the bus out to the game. We checked in, and I went up to my room with Dalton Jones, and I said: "Roomie, this organization has a reputation! How the heck could they schedule us here?"

We changed into our uniforms, went back downstairs, and to get to the team bus we had to walk through the casino. And there were six guys in there at the craps tables—in Red Sox uniforms! Dick Radatz, Dave Morehead, Lee Thomas, and I don't remember who else, all throwing dice! I said to myself, "Oh, my God," and then Billy Herman arrived. Even Herman had his limits. He saw them gambling, turned red, started spitting on the carpet, and began yelling.

"Get them out of there before somebody sees them and starts taking pictures!" he screamed.

A couple of days later, we were in Salt Lake City for another exhibition, and about five of the pitchers spent half the night wandering the streets looking for a bar. They finally ended up standing in front of the Mormon Tabernacle, complaining: "Aren't there *any* bars in this goddamn town?"

THE PRODIGY

I was surprised when the Red Sox handed me the shortstop job. I was only 21, had played only three seasons in the minors, and hadn't exactly lit up Triple-A pitching the previous summer. Naturally, Eddie Bressoud wasn't pleased about having his job taken away, and I couldn't blame him. Bressoud was a six-year veteran who hadn't shown much pop in the National League when the Red Sox got him. The Houston Colt .45s took him from the San Francisco Giants in the expansion draft in 1961 and then quickly swapped him to the Red Sox for shortstop Don Buddin, whose legendary fielding lapses had made him a favorite whipping boy for Boston fans.

Bressoud had given the Red Sox three pretty good years. In 1962 he hit .277 with 40 doubles, nine triples, 14 homers, and scored 79 runs while driving in 68—although he did lead the league's shortstops in errors with 28. He hit 20 homers in 1963, adding 23 doubles and six triples while batting .260. In 1964, he started the season with a 20-game hitting streak and finished at .293 with 41 doubles, 15 homers, 86 runs, and 55 RBIs while also walking 72 times. He had cut down on his errors every year, and at the age of 32, there was no reason for him to believe his job was in jeopardy.

Eddie was actually a pretty good guy, but every time I tried to talk to him, he'd just walk away. I understood that. He wanted to play. He deserved to play. Billy Herman managed to get him into 107 games in 1965, 86 of them at shortstop. But he hit only .226, and the Red Sox traded him to the New York Mets after the season. Two years later Eddie Bressoud was out of baseball.

Not all the Red Sox veterans were as resentful as Bressoud. Frank Malzone, a three-time Gold Glover at third base and eight-time All-Star, played next to me. Malzy was 35 years old and in his last year with the Red Sox, but he helped me out a lot.

I played 103 games that year, 93 of them at shortstop. I hit 13 homers but again didn't hit for much of an average, batting .232. I had hit the ball the other way a lot when I was in the minors, but the Red Sox wanted me to take advantage of The Wall by pulling the ball, hitting home runs, and knocking in runs. When you try to pull everything, you're going to have a hard time hitting for average. But the Red Sox encouraged me to keep doing that, and they were happy with my defense, although I made 19 errors.

Eddie Bressoud was a productive shortstop for the Red Sox from 1962-64 and was naturally resentful when I took his job in 1965. *(Courtesy of the Boston Red Sox)*

EMPTY STATS

My insignificant offensive contributions aside, the Red Sox were a decent-hitting team in 1965. We led the league in both slugging percentage and on-base percentage, and in home runs (165). We were second in hitting and in runs scored. Tony C., only 20 years old, became the youngest player in baseball history to lead the league in homers, belting 32. Yaz (.536) and Tony (.512) finished one-two in the league in slugging percentage. Yaz also led the league in on-base percentage (.398) and tied with Minnesota's Zoilo Versalles—who was the Most Valuable Player that year—for the lead in doubles with 45. Yaz also finished second to Minnesota's Tony Oliva in the batting race, hitting .312. Felix Mantilla's homers dropped from 30 to 18, but he drove in 92 runs and finished fourth in the league in that department.

Still, the Red Sox lost 100 games. Not since 1932, the year before Mr. Yawkey bought the club, had the Red Sox lost that many games. Heck, until the previous season, the Red Sox had never even experienced a 90-loss season during the Yawkey Era. Instead of getting better, things were getting worse!

As many runs as we scored in 1965, we gave up 122 more, more than any team in the league. Defensively, we didn't cover much ground, and the pitching staff wasn't in synch yet. We had a lot of very hard throwers, but Dave Morehead and Jim Lonborg were both young and still learning how to pitch in the big leagues. Bill Monbouquette—who had won 20 games for the Red Sox only two years earlier, had once struck out 17 batters in a game, and had thrown a no-hitter—was now on the downside of his career. Monbo and Morehead tied for the league lead in losses with 18, and Lonnie lost 17. Earl Wilson was still in his prime, but Dennis Bennett, the guy Higgins had traded Stuart to get, had arm troubles and won just five games. Throwing 414 stressful innings out of the bullpen from 1962–64 had also caught up to "The Monster," Dick Radatz. Although Radatz was only 28 years old, he began to break down in 1965 and within another year, he would be just trying to hang on in the majors, going from team to team like a gypsy. By 1969, he would be completely finished.

I'm sure those pitchers got frustrated when we made errors and didn't get to balls. Then somebody would hit one out—it was tough.

As for me, Jim Lonborg, and Dalton Jones, we got a lot of valuable experience. We learned what the major leagues were all about, and that experience was going to help us later.

BOTTOMING OUT

You wouldn't guess it from our final record, but we actually got off to a quick start in 1965, winning four of our first five games. At the end of May, we were still playing .500 ball at 21–21 and were only six games out of first place, but then we fell apart. We lost 13 times in a stretch of 15 games, including eight in a row. After winning a couple from the Washington Senators, we lost nine of the next ten; and by early July, we found ourselves 20 games under .500 at 30–50. Thank goodness, the Senators were in the league. We beat them 10–1, then dropped nine of the next 11.

From May 31 until September 5, the Red Sox never won more than two games in a row. It was disheartening. Every time we won a game, we'd say: "Okay, maybe we're not that bad; we'll put together a winning streak." The next day we'd lose, then lose five in a row. We had some decent players, but as a team, we were just terrible. Period.

Our last series of the season was against the Yankees at Fenway Park. In 1949, the Red Sox played the Yankees in a season-ending two-game series at Yankee Stadium needing one win to clinch the pennant. They lost both. Now we needed to win only one of two to avoid losing 100 games. We lost both. The Yankees weren't even that much better than the Red Sox in 1965. That was the year their dynasty ended, and they were only 75–85 when we played them at the end of the season.

A TWIN HEX

Our record would not have been anywhere near that ugly if we just could have beaten the Minnesota Twins a few times. The Twins had some powerful teams in the mid-1960s, and in 1965, they ended the Yankees' five-year stranglehold on first place and won the pennant with a 102–60 record.

The Twins went 17–1 against us in 1965, and they clobbered us almost every time. Eleven times they scored eight or more runs against us, including a 17–5 rout the first time we played them that year.

The only game we beat them, we won because their third baseman, Frank Kostro, booted a double-play ball that should have ended the seventh inning but led to our only two runs. Dave Morehead threw a three-hitter but walked the bases loaded in the ninth inning. Dick Radatz had to come in and strike out the last two guys, and we won 2–0. The Twins sent Kostro back to the minors right after that. I guess that's how unforgivable it was to lose to the Red Sox in 1965.

We helped the Twins win the pennant that year. They had a good team, but we just couldn't beat them. We'd score a few runs; they'd come back; and then we'd make an error. That's how we lost. We lost ugly. We really did. And we lost *a lot* of games—not just to the Twins, but to everybody.

VALUABLE EXPERIENCE

Even though we had a terrible year as a team, all those losses did nothing to dim my enthusiasm, or that of the other young kids on the club. It was exciting to be in the big leagues and play against all these teams for the first time.

We were also able to make first-hand comparisons. We looked at other teams, the good teams like the Twins, and saw what kind of players they had: players with more ability, players who made fewer mistakes. The Red Sox had some guys with good individual statistics, but never enough of them to put together a team good enough to win. We knew we needed more talent, better players than we had, to win pennants.

Despite our enthusiasm, it wasn't easy to come to Fenway Park in 1965. It was very disheartening. We were the laughingstock of the American League, and rightly so. We'd come off the road, and the people who did show up at Fenway Park were nasty. The crowds were so small that you could hear everything they yelled at us, and most of it was negative. We were just meat for the wolves. At the end of September, when we were closing in on 100 losses, we played two games against the California Angels that drew 461 and 409 fans, respectively.

Red Sox fans wanted us to win, of course, but they were frustrated, and who could blame them? So most didn't bother to come at all. We drew 652,201 fans that year, down nearly a quarter of a million from the previous season! You couldn't give tickets away—nobody wanted them.

Imagine if the Red Sox ever had a team like that now.

THE CHANGING OF THE GUARD

Morehead threw the greatest game of his career on September 16 that year against Cleveland's Luis Tiant, who would become the ace of the Red Sox staff a decade later. Tiant threw extremely hard in those days, and he struck out 11 guys while walking nobody and surrendering just six hits. Morehead, though, who took a 9–16

The direction of the Red Sox franchise turned around 180 degrees when owner Tom Yawkey (right) named Dick O'Connell as general manager in September of 1965. (*Courtesy of the Boston Red Sox*)

record into the game that afternoon, was even sharper. He threw a no-hitter at the Indians. A leadoff walk to Rocky Colavito in the second inning was the only blemish that kept it from being a perfect game. My roomie, Dalton Jones, tripled home a run in the sixth, and first baseman Lee Thomas clubbed his 20th homer of the season in the seventh to account for the only runs off Tiant. Only 1,247 fans showed up at Fenway Park to see the game.

Yet, the biggest accomplishment that day was not Morehead's no-hitter. After the game, Mr. Yawkey fired Mike Higgins as general manager and gave the job to Dick O'Connell. It couldn't have been an easy decision. Higgins had been a part of the Red Sox for almost as long as Mr. Yawkey owned the team, and they were drinking buddies. But putting O'Connell in charge meant the Country Club Era was over.

O'Connell had an entirely different outlook. He liked younger, more aggressive players. He was active, on the phone all the time, making things happen. And, most importantly, he didn't think he was smarter than everybody else. He didn't have a big ego. He did what a general manager is supposed to do: generally manage. He surrounded himself with good baseball people, listened to their advice, and weighed the information he was given before making his decision. More often than not, he made the right one.

After the season ended, Haywood Sullivan was brought in to be the director of player personnel, another good move. Sully had just managed the Kansas City Athletics, the only team in the American League worse than us. He had taken over for Mel McGaha 26 games into the season with the club off to a 5–21 start and finished out the year. The A's played a little bit better under Sully, but a field manager was not something he aspired to be.

Sully had been a Red Sox bonus baby back in the early 1950s and a longtime favorite of Mr. Yawkey. He never hit much in the majors, and back problems shortened his catching career. He badly wanted to get into baseball administration, and now

Mr. Yawkey and O'Connell were bringing him back to Boston and giving him that opportunity. Twelve years later, after Mr. Yawkey had passed away, Haywood Sullivan would buy the Red Sox.

For the young kids like me in the Red Sox organization, the change at the top was great news. We knew we would finally get a real chance to play.

1966

Now that Dick O'Connell was running the organization, the Red Sox roster was crowded with rookies and young players in 1966. Joe Foy, 23, was the new third baseman. Foy had been selected as the Most Valuable Player in Class AAA International League in 1965 after hitting .302 with 21 doubles, eight triples, 14 homers, and 73 RBIs for Toronto. *The Sporting News*, baseball's bible, had also named Foy their Minor League Player of the Year.

Our first baseman was George "Boomer" Scott, 22, who hadn't even played Triple-A ball yet. But Boomer had put together an incredible season at Class AA Pittsfield in 1965, not only winning the Eastern League's Triple Crown but leading the league in just about every category imaginable. Boomer led the EL in batting at .319, hits with 167, doubles with 30, triples with nine, homers with 25, runs batted in with 94, total bases with 290, and slugging percentage at .554. He led the league's third basemen in putouts and assists, but he also led the league in errors with 31; so when he got to the big leagues the Red Sox moved him to first base, where he was outstanding defensively and won eight Gold Gloves.

You had to love Boomer. His broad smile revealed a mouth full of gold teeth, and his body was draped in gold jewelry. Later on, he wore a necklace that was made of what appeared to be small seashells. He would tell writers that the charms were actually second basemen's teeth from breaking up double plays.

An unsung hero, third baseman Joe Foy was one of our rookies in 1966 who would play a key role in winning the pennant a year later. (*Courtesy of the Boston Red Sox*)

Mike Ryan, a 24-year-old catcher who had grown up in Haverhill—a city about 25 miles northwest of Boston—had been with us for a few games in 1965 and would now get an opportunity to play regularly. He never hit much, but he could catch and throw. Ryan played basketball to keep himself in shape during the winter and wished baseballs were as big as basketballs.

"It would be nice swinging at one of them," he mused one time. "I get the bat on the ball. But the holes close up fast, and first base is a foot too far."

Pitcher Darrell "Bucky" Brandon was one of the older rookies at 25. O'Connell had scooped him up from the Houston Astros organization, where he had posted a 13–6 record with a 3.30 ERA for their Triple-A team in Oklahoma City in 1965.

THE GROUNDWORK IS LAID

O'Connell had stayed busy in the off-season, combing other teams' rosters for players who might be useful to the Red Sox. In addition to Brandon, one of his best pickups was 25-year-old pitcher Jose Santiago, who had battled injuries and illness throughout his career and hadn't really gotten much of a chance in Kansas City despite a couple of real good minor-league seasons. The A's had outrighted him to Portland, and O'Connell bought his contract from the Triple-A club. O'Connell traded Lee Thomas and Arnold Earley to the Milwaukee Braves for reliever Dan Osinski, who was 32 years old but would become a key member of our bullpen.

In June 1966, just before the trading deadline, O'Connell swung deals for two other veteran pitchers who would be important to us, although one of the swaps was not very popular with Red Sox fans at the time. He traded Dick Radatz, who had had three great seasons out of the bullpen but had lost his fastball, to the Cleveland Indians for Lee Stange. He also picked up reliever

John Wyatt and outfielder Jose Tartabull from the Athletics in exchange for outfielder Jim Gosger and pitchers Ken Sanders and Guido Grilli.

No one could foresee that pieces were falling into place for what would become one of the most improbable pennants in Major League Baseball history.

That wouldn't happen, though, in 1966.

CAN'T STAND THE KIDS

Mike Higgins was gone, but Billy Herman was still managing the club. He was in the second year of a two-year contract, and O'Connell kept him on. I'm sure he must have been unhappy when he was told he had to keep and play the kids. He knew he'd have to win games to keep his job, and I'm sure he was thinking: "Jeez, I've got no chance now. We lost 100 games with the veterans last year, and we'll probably lose 125 with the kids." Right then, I bet he started thinking more about golf than baseball.

Herman got along great with the veteran players we still had. He just didn't feel comfortable with a lot of young players. He was from the old school. He didn't like the way the young players went about things, even though we worked hard at improving our game. We did have a couple of real good coaches, though. Pete Runnels, who had won two batting titles with the Red Sox in 1960 and 1962, was the hitting coach. Sal Maglie, nicknamed "The Barber" for his willingness to pitch inside and intimidate hitters when he was pitching for the New York Giants, was our pitching coach. I'm sure Maglie made a major impression on "Gentleman Jim" Lonborg, who would lead the American League by drilling 19 batters in 1967. Oh, yeah, Lonnie would also win 22 games and the Cy Young Award that year, too.

"Sal's message was simple," Lonborg recalled several decades later. "You want to pitch semi-pro ball, go on and lay it over the plate, hard as you can. You want to win in the majors? Make them afraid you'll stick one in their ear."

BRINGING UP THE BABIES

The atmosphere was totally different in spring training—and not just because the Red Sox had moved their camp back to Florida after 10 years in Arizona. The young players just had far more enthusiasm than the older guys, and they already knew each other from the minors.

We all wanted to do well, of course, and we weren't happy when we didn't. But when we lost, which was pretty often at first, we didn't get too depressed or say we were a lousy team. We knew we had a lot of young, inexperienced guys, and we just told ourselves to keep pushing, that we were going to get better.

We helped each other out. The guys who had already been there for a year or two, like me, Dalton Jones, and Tony C. would tell the rookies what to expect, how somebody was going to pitch them—and they listened. Closeness developed between all of us. We all became good friends. I don't know if we would have hit it off had we all come from different organizations. We had forged a bond before we even got to the big leagues.

HERMAN'S TRADE

Billy Herman never bonded with us, though. In fact, he even tried to engineer a deal behind Dick O'Connell's back to trade Yaz to the Yankees right after the 1965 season. After winning 14 pennants and nine World Series in 16 years from 1949–64, the Yankees had gone 77–85 in 1965. Everybody thought it was just an off year, but the truth was, the Yankees had gotten old.

Herman contacted Yankees GM Ralph Houk, and Houk's eyes must have lit up like fireworks on the Fourth of July when

Herman offered to trade him Yaz in exchange for outfielder Tom Tresh and shortstop Phil Linz. Tresh had been the AL's Rookie of the Year in 1962 and was a pretty good offensive player, a switch-hitter with consistent 20-homer power who was two years older than Yaz. Linz could swing the bat a teeny bit but had no power and was coming off a .207 season in 1965. Yaz was coming off his first 20-homer season in 1965, and Houk knew he'd hit for much more power in Yankee Stadium, where the right-field fence was about 80 feet closer than in Fenway.

Whether Herman thought O'Connell would leap at the deal when it was presented a *fait accompli*, no one will know. He was lucky O'Connell, who turned it down flat, didn't leap at his throat.

What's that old saying about some of the best trades are the ones you don't make? Linz was out of the game by 1969. Tresh started to go downhill in 1966 and was gone a year after Linz. Yaz? He won the Triple Crown in 1967 and played his way into the Hall of Fame.

MEA CULPA

I had my own issues with Herman. I started off the season playing at short, and I struggled. I was overmatched at the plate, and the veteran pitchers set me up. I'd chase bad balls in the dirt, and until I learned to figure it out, I wasn't going to get any better. Then Billy started playing Eddie Bressoud; and if I wasn't playing, I definitely wasn't going to get any better.

Being Italian, I had a temper when I was younger, and we had it out in the dugout one day. He said something like: "Who the hell are you to confront me with something like this? Get the hell out of here!" So I did. I showered and went home while the game was still being played. Billy fined me $2,000, and I was only making $6,000. I was immature, and I handled it wrong. I apologized to Billy and promised him it would never happen again.

O'Connell called me into his office, told me he knew I wasn't making much money, and cut the fine in half. But that was still one-sixth of my salary for the entire season.

THE KIDS ARE ALL RIGHT

Unlike 1964 and 1965, when the Red Sox got off to surprisingly good starts, we got off to a dreadful start in 1966. We lost our first five games—three of them in extra innings—and 14 of 19 before winning two in a row for the first time on May 8. Shockingly, those two wins were a doubleheader sweep of the defending AL champion Minnesota Twins, whom we had beaten just once the previous year. Before we could get too full of ourselves, though, we lost the next six.

We got some great pitching for a week in the middle of May—surrendering just 10 runs while winning six in a row—but we couldn't keep it up. We lost 12 of 14 in early June, and after dropping the first game of a doubleheader to Washington on the Fourth of July, we were 28–51 and in last place, five games behind the ninth-place Senators and 25 ½ games behind the first-place Baltimore Orioles.

And then our fortunes began to change. Lee Stange beat the Senators 1–0 in the second game, and we won nine out of 10. We went 44–39 the rest of the way, and only three teams in the American League had a better record during the second half. We became more experienced, made fewer mistakes, hit the ball better. We made the double play when we needed it, and we started scoring enough runs to win. The pitching wasn't great, but it was okay. We were last in the league in pitching at midseason and remained last when it concluded; but our staff earned-run average over the second half was a respectable fifth in the league. Most importantly, our confidence started to grow. The second half of 1966 was really the beginning of 1967 for us.

Despite our improvement in the second half, Billy Herman didn't seem all that elated. He liked winning well enough, but he wasn't enthusiastic about the way we were winning those games. He didn't like our style, and our second-half record couldn't save his job. O'Connell fired him on September 8 and let Pete Runnels run the club the rest of the way.

Because we had so much trouble winning at the start of the season and finished ninth with a 72–90 record, not very many people noticed or appreciated how much better we played from July 4 on—although attendance at Fenway Park did pick up during the second half. We ended up drawing 811,000 fans, an increase of about 25 percent over 1965.

UNIMPRESSIVE STATS

Individually, no one had a standout season for the Red Sox in 1966. Yaz dipped to .278 with 16 homers and 80 RBIs; and Conigliaro, who had led the league in homers with 32 in 1965, slipped to 28. He did lead the club in RBIs with 93, and rookie first baseman George Scott hit 27 homers with 90 RBIs but batted just .245. Rookie third baseman Joe Foy hit .262 with 15 homers and 63 RBIs and finished second in the league in walks with 91. As for me, I boosted my home run output to 18 but hit only .238 with 59 RBIs. Jose Santiago led the staff in wins with 12, and Jim Lonborg was 10–10.

LOOKING DOWN ON THE YANKEES

Oh yeah, we did accomplish something in 1966 that no Red Sox team had done since 1948: We finished ahead of the Yankees in the standings. We beat out the last-place Yankees by a mere half-game. That thin margin of a half-game, however, was all that prevented us from becoming the first team in major-league history to go from worst to first in the span of a year.

2

SPRING TRAINING

1967

The Red Sox, having broken in two rookies in 1964, two more in 1965, and four in 1966, were going to get still younger in 1967. Second baseman Mike Andrews and center fielder Reggie Smith, a pair of rookies who had gotten into a few games at the end of 1966, were destined to join the lineup, meaning seven of the eight regulars would have three years or less of major-league experience. And Carl Yastrzemski, the "old man" with six years in the big leagues and the senior player on the Red Sox in terms of service, was only 27. The average age of our regular lineup in 1967 would be 23 ½.

Of the four pitchers who would do the bulk of the starting for us in 1967, Jim Lonborg had two years of major-league experience, and Darrell Brandon had one.

General manager Dick O'Connell wanted someone to manage the team who was familiar with the personnel, could teach and motivate the young players, and get the most out of their abilities. That man was 38-year-old Dick Williams, who had managed the top Red Sox farm team, the Toronto Maple Leafs, to Class AAA International League championships in 1965 and 1966. O'Connell hired Williams in late September.

"We were in Boston for the organizational meetings," Williams said, "and Dick O'Connell said he wanted to give Eddie Popowski and me a ride back to the Howard Johnson's near the ballpark, where we were staying. I already knew Pop was going to get a job on the major-league staff, but I didn't know what was in store for me. We got in the car, O'Connell drove around the corner, and stopped. He told me I was the new manager of the Red Sox. He didn't even ask me if I wanted it. He just told me."

I thought Dick Williams was a great choice. Although I had never played for him, I knew him a little bit from playing with him in spring training in 1963 and 1964, and, based on what he

General manager Dick O'Connell (left) made a shrewd decision when he hired Dick Williams to manage the Red Sox in 1967. (*Courtesy of the Boston Red Sox*)

did in Toronto, I was excited. I hadn't seen him manage, but I heard good things about him from the players who had played for him.

One of the things I'd heard was that he'd gotten into a fistfight with a pitcher named Mickey Sinks. Sinks was a big fellow, 6'2" 200 pounds. So I knew Dick was a scrappy guy who wasn't afraid to go at it with anybody.

"Sinks was my closer in Toronto," Williams remembered. "One day he came into my office, which really wasn't much more than a closet, and asked me to recommend him for promotion to the major leagues. I told him I couldn't do that, and he popped me in the left eye. It wasn't much of a fight. Two punches. The one he threw and the one I threw. Yeah, he was a big guy. But he wasn't in very good shape. I hit him in the mid-section, he went down, and that was that."

Dick was also a sarcastic guy. He always spoke like a bench jockey, which is what he was when he broke into the majors with the Brooklyn Dodgers in 1951. He stuck around the majors as a utility guy for 13 years, playing for five different clubs (including the Baltimore Orioles three times), and he knew how to get under a player's skin.

The first time I ran into Williams after he got the manager's job was in January of 1967, the day of the annual Boston Baseball Writers Dinner. A bunch of us were in town for the dinner, and we were hanging around the clubhouse at Fenway Park when Dick sauntered in. The guys who had played for him got real quiet all of a sudden, and Dick went around shaking hands with the rest of us, introducing himself. No smiles, though. He was deadly serious. He started talking about spring training, which was only a few weeks away, and we casually mentioned we'd be in shape when we got there. He snarled: "You better be!"

In those days most players didn't work out year round. The money wasn't anywhere near as good as it is now—even if you were playing for the Red Sox—and a lot of players had to work at off-season jobs to make ends meet. Most players didn't start working out lightly until January. The purpose of spring training back then was to get in shape, to lose the 15 or 20 pounds you might have put on over the winter. But Williams made it clear to us that day that he expected us to already be in shape by the time we got to Winter Haven, that he planned to devote spring training to drills and teaching and not wasting time watching us sweat our way into playing shape. He told each of us what our weight should be when we arrived, which would be our playing weight for the season, and most of us complied.

Williams wanted a hard-working coaching staff that was also well acquainted both with him and the kids who had come up through the organization. He retained Sal Maglie as the pitching coach, but Pete Runnels was let go. Red Sox great Bobby Doerr, who had been an instructor in the minors with the organization for a decade, was brought in to serve as the hitting coach. Eddie Popowski, who had been in the organization for three decades and had managed some of the youngsters in Double-A ball, including me, would be Williams' right-hand man and coach third base. Al Lakeman was the bullpen coach.

"If they have any hard times, I should know what mistakes they made as kids and how they've fallen back into them," Doerr said.

"When they need a pat on the back, they'll get it," Popowski said. "And when they deserve a boot in the fanny, they'll get that, too."

WE'RE STILL A JOKE

The press thought that Williams, who had played for the Country Club Red Sox at the end of his career, was all bluster, and that nothing was going to change. A week before spring training began, *Boston Globe* columnist Bud Collins wrote: "Another endless summer for Uncle Tom's Townies begins Saturday morning when recreation director Dick Williams asks them to try to touch their toes a few times and throw the baseball around just to get the feel of things. He won't ask them to do anything hard right away, like catching the baseball. They will have trouble doing that in August, and to ask it of them now would only break their spirits before the season has begun."

MEET THE PRESS

The writers were surprised and even a little miffed when Williams didn't have a lot of time to spend with them during spring training. They were accustomed to sitting around with Red Sox managers for hours on end, usually over drinks, and shooting the breeze. But when Williams wasn't on the field barking instructions (and insults), he was usually in closed-door meetings with his coaching staff going over the training regimen. Williams also barred the writers from traveling on the team bus to exhibition games, telling them he wanted to use the bus as a rolling classroom.

"Williams has a schedule mapped out for them that looks like something out of West Point," wrote the *Globe's* Clif Keane. Williams, with his brush-cut hair, looked like a Marine drill sergeant and certainly talked like one.

Williams didn't really do any teaching on those bus trips. But he wanted to be able to yell at us when we messed up without worrying about what he said being printed in the Boston papers.

In his meetings with the press, Williams insisted we were going to work incessantly on fundamentals. "We'll do that stuff until they really get tired of it," he said. "I want my men to hit to right field a lot. I like to play baseball, not Fenway Park baseball. I want the same game played in all parks. The hitters will have to look for signs on every pitch. In the past there haven't been many things going on. But there'll be more things going on for this club this year."

VOLLEYBALL, ANYONE?

One of Williams' innovations to improve conditioning was to have the pitchers play volleyball during spring training. The writers got a good chuckle out of that. How could playing volleyball improve anybody's baseball skills? Ted Williams, for once in his life, agreed with the writers. "Volleyball! What the hell is going on here!" he bellowed when he arrived in Winter Haven to work with the hitters.

The pitchers thought it was punishment at first. Instead of going to the corner and putting on a dunce cap, they had to go play volleyball. But after a while they actually had fun doing it.

"Maybe all we'll wind up with is the best volleyball team in Florida," Williams conceded. But he didn't really believe that, even if the press wanted to speculate the Red Sox might have a brighter future in volleyball than baseball.

THE WILLIAMS MANIFESTO

At 9:30 a.m. on Saturday morning, February 27, 1966, Dick Williams called a team meeting on the field before the first formal workout of the spring.

"We're going to work hard on fundamentals on this team. Our pitchers are going to do a lot of running," he vowed. "I have no set ideas on the men who will make this team. There are a lot of jobs open around here. Names mean nothing. Performance counts all the way with me."

Williams didn't want us thinking strictly about home runs, long the hallmark of the Red Sox, and we knew he meant business. He wanted us to stay out of slumps by hitting the ball up the middle more, something I always did anyway when I started trying to pull the ball too much. We were going to hit and run. We were going to bunt and run. We were going to steal bases. We were going to do things that would help us win, and if we didn't do them, we weren't going to play, no matter who we were. That comment was directed mostly at Carl Yastrzemski, Tony Conigliaro, and George Scott. And during the season he did take Tony C. and Boomer out of the lineup when they didn't do what he wanted. The exception was Yaz, although not early in the 1967 season. But when Yaz started hitting all those home runs in May, Williams let him be. Dick didn't want to have him bunting when it was more beneficial to the team to let him try to hit it out of the ballpark.

Believe it or not, those things are fun to do instead of just standing up there and swinging away. Even the veterans, like Don Demeter, Jose Tartabull, and Bob Tillman, bought into it, although veteran outfielder George Thomas quipped after Williams' speech: "Just looking around here, I would dare say that the only person sure to go north with this team would be Ricky Williams."

Ricky was the manager's 10-year-old son, who had been making an impression on the players in camp with his baseball ability. (Ricky would become a minor-league pitcher when he grew up.)

"Basically he told us we'd either win or we'd get traded," said Dalton Jones.

It was definitely a different speech than the Red Sox had been accustomed to hearing in spring training. Billy Herman's speech was something like: "Let's have fun, and be sure to hit the ball straight when you're playing golf."

Williams had his work cut out for him. "I spent 2 ½ days with them going over everything on that field, right down to the on-deck circle," he said. "Some of them didn't even know what the double lines up the first-base line were for."

Maybe the Red Sox weren't putting a lot of pressure on Williams to win right away. But he was putting pressure on himself.

"My wife, Norma, and I took a three-year lease on an apartment in Peabody, and we bought the furniture on a three-year installment plan," he explained later. "I was only on a one-year contract. So if I was going to go down, I was going to go down my way."

A VETERAN'S VIEWPOINT

Even our veteran players seemed to welcome the new approach and the hard work.

After one vigorous workout, well-traveled reliever Don McMahon, soaking with sweat, said it was the most organized camp he'd ever attended. The Red Sox were the 37-year-old reliever's fourth major-league team.

"I think this is something the Red Sox needed," he said. "The worst camp I was ever in was when I was with the (Milwaukee) Braves. We had only one field, and players stood around half the day. You could sneak away for an hour and a half and never be missed. Honest!"

And then he added slyly: "But we won the pennant both years."

WILLIAMS IN CHARGE

The press was curious to see if Dick Williams would kowtow to the team's two best young studs, Carl Yastrzemski and Tony Conigliaro, and extend them preferential treatment. None of the previous Red Sox managers had been able to exert much control over the two ultra-talented outfielders.

Williams had already antagonized Yaz at least once before, back when they were playing together. Like I mentioned earlier, the abrasive Williams loved to needle players, and one day he sidled up to Yaz and said: "You run the bases just like Jackie Robinson. Only you get caught." Yaz was not amused.

Then one of Williams' first acts as manager had been to strip Yaz of his captaincy. Billy Herman had named Yaz the team captain the previous year. Williams wanted it clear to everyone that there was only going to be one chief on the Red Sox, and it was going to be him.

"This club has become a cruise ship overrun with captains and players thinking they are captain," he told us. "The cruise is over, and you don't need a captain anymore. You have a new boss now: me."

I don't think Williams did it to cut Yaz down to size. I think he figured that taking the captain's responsibilities away would allow Yaz to concentrate fully on playing ball.

The second day of camp, the day after Williams' my-way-or-you-won't-play speech, Yaz asked for a private meeting with the skipper. Uh-oh. But after emerging, Yaz met with the writers. "I told him I had the reputation of not getting along with managers, and I didn't want him to think I was that way," Yaz said. "I told him that what he wanted me to do, I would do every second. If he wants a bunt, he'll get a bunt. A chop to move a man ahead, and he'll get it. I told him I would be the most cooperative guy around, and I will."

Yaz went from captain to cheerleader that spring, talking to guys and telling them that the things Williams wanted us to do were really going to help this ball club. That was important because here was the guy who was the star of the team agreeing with the manager and endorsing his methods.

I had gone through two tough years with the Red Sox, losing 190 games. It had been a lot worse for Yaz, who had played six years in Boston while losing an average of almost 90 games a year. He was tired of losing. He wanted to win, and he'd do anything Dick wanted to improve the ball club.

Even in a posed spring training photo, Carl Yastrzemski is a picture of concentration. A focused Yaz would win the Triple Crown and be the American League MVP in 1967. (*Courtesy of the Boston Red Sox*)

Getting Conigliaro to toe the line was a bit trickier. All unmarried players, or married players who were not accompanied by their families to spring training, were required to live at the team hotel in Winter Haven. Tony, who had girlfriends everywhere, had a clause written into his contract that he did not have to stay at the team hotel, and when he saw the Haven Hotel, a stucco monstrosity past its prime, he definitely did not want to stay there.

Even if Tony had been a monk, I could understand why he wouldn't have wanted to stay at the Haven. No self-respecting monk would have wanted to stay there, and no one on the Red Sox wanted to stay there, either. It was a dump, a really decrepit place. It smelled, and when you turned on the shower, cockroaches would come streaming out of the nozzle. After living there for a couple of weeks I couldn't take it anymore. I called my wife and said: "Baby, get down here and bring the kid! Take the next plane! I don't know where we're going to stay, but I'm not staying here!"

But Tony wasn't married, and Williams would not grant him an exemption. Finally the two of them hashed it over with Dick O'Connell. Tony, to his credit, relented and agreed to room at the Haven with the other single players. Now Dick Williams had everyone on the team in line.

THE FIRST TEST OF AUTHORITY

Well, almost everyone. On the third day of camp, Williams' authority was challenged for the first time when pitchers Dennis Bennett and Bob Sadowski showed up 25 minutes late for the 10 a.m. workout. Bennett told the manager they hadn't received the wake-up call they'd left at the front desk. We all raised our eyebrows when we heard that excuse. We knew their reputation. To our surprise, Williams accepted their excuse but warned them he would not tolerate lateness in the future.

As if the 12:30 curfew instituted by Williams wasn't already unpopular with the players who enjoyed the nightlife, now he left orders at the Haven Hotel for the desk clerks to wake up all the players at 7 a.m. The other players knew Bennett would never get up that early and would try to sleep in, so they rang his room repeatedly to annoy him.

A BAD FIRST IMPRESSION

We played our first intrasquad game on March 8, and Dick Williams was appalled at how often we messed up fundamental plays. Several times he stopped the game and screamed at us.

"We will keep right on talking about fundamentals," Williams told the press afterward. "The game shouldn't be this tough for these men. You lose games through those little mistakes, and we can't afford to be giving away anything to anyone."

THE ROOKIES

When Dick Williams talked about a lot of jobs being open on the 1967 Red Sox, two of them were center field and second base.

O'Connell had traded his best pitcher, Earl Wilson, to the Detroit Tigers the previous May in exchange for center fielder Don Demeter. The 31-year-old Demeter had hit more than 20 homers each year from 1961–64, including 1962 when he hit .307 with 29 homers and 107 RBIs for the Philadelphia Phillies. But Demeter was on the shadowed down slope of the hill by '66, and while he hit .292 for the Red Sox, he produced only nine homers and 29 RBIs in 73 games. Wilson, meanwhile had gone 13–6 with a 2.59 ERA for the Tigers in 1966 and would be a 22-game winner in 1967. O'Connell got snookered on that deal. But he was new at the game, and he would get a lot better at it.

Demeter knew what he was up against right away in spring training when Williams declared his preference for 22-year-old rookie Reggie Smith.

"If he shows me he belongs there, the position is Smith's," Williams said.

Carl Reginald Smith was a switch-hitter with great speed. He had all the tools, including, as Red Sox scout Mace Brown said, "the best arm I'd ever seen on a human," although he often had no idea where the ball was going when he let it go. Smith was a shortstop when the Red Sox drafted him off Minnesota's roster in 1963, and the Red Sox tried to convert him into a third baseman

Ultra-talented and switch-hitting center fielder Reggie Smith was one of the rookies who helped us win the pennant in 1967. (*Courtesy of the Boston Red Sox*)

during spring training in 1964. "They never sold any first-base box seats that year," Smith said. "The people were too scared to sit there the way I threw the ball over to first."

The Red Sox made him an outfielder instead. Playing for Williams in Toronto in 1966, Smith led the International League in hitting with a .320 average while blasting 30 doubles and 18 homers and driving in 80 runs. He clouted five more homers during the playoffs. Williams knew first-hand what Smith was capable of doing.

Second base was a bigger problem for the Red Sox. Neither Dalton Jones, an $80,000 bonus baby, nor George Smith had hit well enough to keep the position. Twenty-three-year-old Mike Andrews had hit 14 homers for Toronto in 1966, but just as impressive in Williams' estimation was that he also led the IL in sacrifice bunts. Some people thought Andrews, a converted shortstop who stood 6'3" and weighed 195 pounds, was too big to play second. Bobby Doerr, one of the greatest-fielding second basemen of all time, disagreed.

"He's a natural," Doerr insisted. "He doesn't look like one of those smooth second basemen only because he's so tall. Don't let the looks fool you. He can do it all, the double play, all of it."

George Smith, meanwhile, took himself out of the equation in the early days of spring training when he tore the cartilage in his knee during a rundown drill and had to undergo season-ending surgery. He never played in the majors again.

Then Andrews' back got so sore, he couldn't bend over to pick up a ground ball. It turned out he had injured his back lifting weights during the winter but hadn't told anybody. Williams was furious when he found out Andrews might not be ready for the start of the season and said if he'd known he was hurt, he never would have brought him to camp. With George Smith and Andrews out, the only option seemed to be the versatile Jones, and Williams thought he was more valuable as a utility infielder.

But the Red Sox did have depth in center field, where Demeter and Jose Tartabull could platoon. So just before the end of spring training, he put Reggie Smith at second. Despite his scatter-armed reputation, Reggie did a passable job there and was our second baseman on Opening Day.

THE NEW YAZ

Yaz, often criticized in Boston for not hitting home runs the way Ted Williams had, talked about changing his approach to hitting in the spring of 1967. It sounded like he had bought into Dick Williams' philosophy lock, stock, and barrel.

"I'm going to drag bunt for base hits," he said. "I'm sick and tired of hitting one-hop line drives to the second baseman, who is laying back. If I can learn to bunt, I'll make the infielders honest. I'm going to drag bunt at least once in every exhibition game."

Yaz may have been absolutely serious when he made that statement. But everyone was glad it was quickly forgotten, because Yaz put together one of the greatest all-around years in baseball history in the summer of 1967. He won the Triple Crown, leading the league in batting (.326), runs (112), hits (189), homers (44), RBIs (121), total bases (360), slugging percentage (.622), and on-base percentage (.421).

Yaz showed up that spring in the best shape of his career. He had devoted his first few off-seasons to earning a degree at Merrimack College, but now he was finished with school. He committed himself body and soul to Gene Berde, a physiotherapist at the Colonial Country Club in Lynnfield, Massachusetts. Berde, a refugee who had once trained the Hungarian Olympic boxing team, put Yaz through a strenuous 90-minute workout six days a week.

"You think you in shape? You, the big baseball player?" he told Yaz. "You can't even run a hundred yards. You no athlete. I make you athlete." And he did.

"I was skipping rope for 10 minutes straight, and then I was sprinting until I thought my lungs would burst," Yaz said. "He gave me every exercise, except lifting weights, that anybody ever heard of, and he made me do them. Soon I was feeling better than I ever have in my life, and I put on six pounds! Got up to 185 and felt so strong. I've only lost one pound since we got here."

Yaz also made some key adjustments at the plate that spring. He had hit only .198 against lefthanded pitchers in 1966, and on the first day of workouts the great Ted Williams suggested he close his batting stance.

"Ted told me to close the hip, and I went right to work on it. I can't see as much of the ball, but I'm not helping the pitcher, either. This way I can wait and have more leverage. I know I'm hitting better, and Bobby Doerr keeps reminding me if I slip back to the old way."

Yaz learned to pull the ball that spring. He could get to those inside pitches now and pound them with authority. He still practiced bunting more than ever, because he wanted to win. But we weren't very deep into the season before Yaz began blossoming into one of the greatest power hitters of his generation.

SAME OLD SOX . . . JUST YOUNGER

We played our first exhibition game on March 10 against the Chicago White Sox at Payne Park in Sarasota. It was a disaster right from the start.

White Sox rookie Ed Stroud led off the bottom of the first inning by drawing a walk from Dennis Bennett, then stole second as rookie catcher Russ Gibson—getting his first real chance to make the club after 10 years in the minors—heaved the ball into center field for an error. Rifle-armed Reggie Smith charged in to retrieve the ball as Stroud streaked for third, and he overthrew

Carl Yastrzemski changed his hitting style in the spring of 1967 and became one of the most feared sluggers in baseball. (*Courtesy of the Boston Red Sox*)

the bag so badly he planted the ball 10 feet up on a screen that protected the fans in the third-base grandstand. Stroud scored on that error, and the White Sox clobbered us 8–3. We made four errors that day.

"That ball was a hot potato out there, wasn't it?" a surprisingly light-hearted Dick Williams said afterward.

The press was less forgiving. Ray Fitzgerald wrote in the *Boston Globe* the next morning: "There's a new manager, there's a new body in center field, another at second base, and still another behind the plate. But cut away all the trimmings and it seemed like the same old Red Sox . . ."

Five days later, in a 5–4 loss to the White Sox, both Jose Tartabull and Tony Horton committed blunders on the basepaths and were thrown out.

Fitzgerald wrote: "Dick Williams keeps talking about fundamental baseball, but evidently he's speaking in Swahili, because the Red Sox keep running the bases like the Katzenjammer Kids."

This time Williams wasn't as forgiving.

"We went over baserunning for an hour and a half yesterday, and we'll do it again when we get back to Winter Haven," he promised. "We'll just go over and over these mistakes until we don't make them."

THE BOOMER

Dick Williams kept George Scott off balance all through spring training. Part of it must have been motivational, because Boomer had a tendency to get complacent from time to time. But Boomer was also a natural-born baseball player with tremendous instincts, and Williams wanted to see if he could turn all that potential versatility into an asset that would benefit the team. He talked about playing Scott at third base, his original position when the Red Sox signed him. He talked about playing Scott in the outfield.

He even talked about playing him at second base! But Boomer was stubborn; he only wanted to play first base.

Joe Foy missed the first part of spring training with a shoulder injury, and Williams played Scott at third. This also gave him an opportunity to get a real good look at Tony Horton at first base. Horton had hit .297 with 26 homers and 85 RBIs for Williams at Toronto the previous summer, but he could only play first base, and even that not very well. He tried, but he wasn't very good.

Horton had played 60 games for us in 1965, my rookie year. One game in Baltimore he was chasing a foul pop and somehow ended up getting stuck under the rolled-up tarp at Memorial Stadium. It took about 45 minutes to extract him. They almost had to send for a crane to lift the thing. A few days after that he tried to catch a line drive, and it hit him right in the kneecap and put him out for three weeks. Billy Herman said he'd never seen that happen before, somebody getting hit in the knee while trying to catch a line drive.

Still, Williams was reluctant to write off Horton and give the first base job outright to Scott. Williams was probably listening to Bobby Doerr, who kept telling the press that Horton might be the next Harmon Killebrew.

Foy returned to the lineup in mid-March, and in his first exhibition game—a wild 23–18 victory over the New York Mets in St. Petersburg—he banged out four hits, including a triple, drew two walks, and knocked in five runs. Boomer, happy to be playing first base again, also had a great day, getting a homer, two doubles, a single, and a walk.

In the ninth inning, while we were putting together a 10-run inning to rally from an 18–13 deficit, Foy, who was scheduled to bat next, dawdled in the on-deck circle as Boomer ambled out from the dugout.

"How many hits you got?" Foy asked as the plate umpire motioned impatiently for him to get into the batter's box.

"I got three now. I'll get the fourth," Boomer replied.

George "Boomer" Scott finished fourth in the batting race with a .303 average and won a Gold Glove at first base for us in 1967. (*Courtesy of the Boston Red Sox*)

"When was the last time you had four hits in a game?"

"Can't remember."

"You got them because you're playing where you ought to play," Foy told him with a chuckle. "Get right back there and play where you're supposed to play. Stop foolin' around with my job."

"I don't want your job," Boomer assured him. "You keep it and let me keep mine. We'll both hit."

But a few days later Williams decided to play Scott in right field in order to get another look at Horton. Boomer didn't want to play there and complained about it to Eddie Popowski. Williams and Popowski cleverly had a good cop-bad cop routine going, and Pop was the good cop.

"This is going to ruin my hitting," Boomer whined.

"How can playing right field ruin your hitting? The man is trying to let you get some swings," Popowski argued.

Shortly before the game, Williams and Scott crossed paths.

"I'm not a right fielder," Boomer told him.

"You are today," Williams declared.

Two days later Scott was in right field in a game against the Los Angeles Dodgers in Winter Haven when John Kennedy belted a ball to right that Boomer misjudged. Seeing the ball was going to get over his head, Scott turned around and ran face-first into the unpadded cinderblock wall at Chain O' Lakes Park.

"He moved the wall from 330 feet to 332," Mike Andrews quipped.

The impact knocked Scott out cold for more than a minute. We all thought he was dead.

"That's a very long time," said our trainer, Buddy LeRoux. "Look at Zora Folley against Clay. He got knocked out but was back up on his feet in 10 or 12 seconds."

Cassius Clay, as Muhammad Ali was called back then, had kayoed Folley in a heavyweight fight the previous night.

Scott suffered a concussion and a sprained wrist and would miss a few days of training. Williams, however, was unapologetic about sticking Boomer in the outfield, saying: "Scott has good baseball instincts and can play anywhere. Horton's only chance is at first."

Williams said his one regret was playing Scott in right field, and he would only play him in left field in the future.

"Isn't the left-field wall as hard as the right-field wall?" one of the writers asked.

"Yes, but it's easier to judge a fly in left than in right, and he won't feel so strange," Williams explained.

We didn't tell it to the press, but we agreed with them. We couldn't understand why Williams was playing Scott in the outfield. Boomer was a great athlete, but he wasn't an outfielder. In fact, he went on to play 2,034 games in the major leagues, and not one of them was in the outfield.

ANOTHER INJURY FOR TONY C.

We also lost Tony Conigliaro to an injury on March 18 when John Wyatt broke his shoulder blade with a pitch during batting practice. But it could have been much, much worse.

The Red Sox flew Tony back to Boston for X-rays and an examination by the club physician, Dr. Tom Tierney. Fortunately, it was only a hairline fracture, and Tony would be playing again before the end of spring training.

It was the fifth time he'd broken a bone in some part of his body, and he hadn't even played five seasons yet. His dad, Sal, couldn't figure it out.

"I can't understand all these injuries happening to Tony," he said. "He played football four years in high school and never was hurt."

Little did we all know then that all those broken bones were merely minor interruptions to his career compared to the tragedy that would befall him five months later to the day after he broke his scapula.

A NEW RESPONSIBILITY

Dick Williams never got on me a lot. When I made a mistake, he'd let me know. But he didn't dwell on it or punish me for it. And he was that way with most of the guys.

Williams had abolished the role of captain when he relieved Carl Yastrzemski of that duty after being named manager of the Red Sox. But near the end of spring training he called the infielders together and told them he was making me captain of the infield. "If Rico wants to move you, you move," he told them. "It's the same as having me out there telling you." I was the most experienced guy in the infield, but I was only 23 years old, and that was the first time anyone had ever shown that kind of confidence in me. It worked wonders for me and my career.

THE PREDICTION

We were winning more than we lost during the Grapefruit League season. In 1966 we had lost our first eight exhibition games and left Florida with an 8–19 record. It's true that wins and losses don't really mean anything in spring training, and we were still making some glaring mistakes, which the press never failed to ignore. But we knew we were playing better baseball than we ever had, and we knew we were going to get better. Even the Yankees, who had plenty of troubles of their own, recognized that when we beat them 5–2 in Winter Haven on March 22. Yaz blasted a homer and a double in that game, and I hit one out, too.

After the game Mickey Mantle, who was nearing the end of his career, praised us. "They'll be tough," he predicted, "the way they used to be when things were better. That might be a real good ball club if they get pitching. They've got everything else."

The Boston writers dutifully printed Mantle's comments. I don't think they believed him, though. At the end of spring training, I don't think any of the Boston writers picked us to finish higher than sixth. The consensus around baseball was that the Red Sox were a ninth-place team again, and the odds-makers in Las Vegas made us 100–1 shots to win the pennant.

"I don't care if they pick us for last," Williams said on March 26, four days after Mantle had complimented us. "My first year in Toronto we were picked to finish last, and we finished third. We fooled them again last year. Where they pick us is a big joke.

"The Red Sox have had a lot of individual players playing for themselves," Williams said of the recent past. "We're going as a unit this year. It helps to have a compatible group. I like the club. The players are battling, hustling, and going for each other. I honestly believe we'll win more games than we lose."

We were still raw and prone to mistakes, but Williams had seen something in us we couldn't even see in ourselves yet.

"There was talent there to win if they applied themselves, and the guys I had brought with me from Toronto already knew the way I operated," Williams said later. "But they had to learn to believe in themselves."

I don't know if we really paid much attention to our won-loss record that spring, or thought about how high we'd finish in the standings when the season began. But we did know we were playing better baseball than we ever had, and that was our focus: playing better. When Dick said that we'd win more often than we'd lose, we believed him. But, honestly, we weren't thinking about winning the pennant. We were thinking about winning enough games to finish in the first division, somewhere in the middle of the pack. We knew that wasn't an impossible dream.

Williams reiterated his prediction on April 7, the last day of spring training. His comment got even more attention then. All the Boston papers printed it, and everybody back home guffawed.

But we were going to have the last laugh.

3

APRIL 1967

I would love to tell you that Dick Williams had taught us well, and we were ready to play a winning brand of baseball when the regular season began. The truth was that we hadn't quite mastered all the fundamentals yet, and we played some pretty bad games in the first few weeks.

Everybody thinks you're supposed to learn all those fundamentals when you're in the minor leagues, and we had. But it's a whole different environment in the big leagues. You're playing against better players, and you have to relearn everything. For example, in the minors you might be bunting against a guy throwing 88 miles an hour. In the majors you're trying to do it against a guy throwing 93 with much better stuff, much more movement on the ball. Guys ran faster, and the fielders had more range. You hit a ball on the ground to the left side in Baltimore when Brooks Robinson and Luis Aparicio, and later Mark Belanger, were there, you were lucky to get a hit. You had to do everything faster, and when you're learning to do that, you will make mistakes.

OPENING DAY

It didn't help that the weather that spring was unusually cold and windy. Opening Day, April 11, was postponed because it was 35 degrees with a 40-mph wind blowing, and when we played the next afternoon, the conditions weren't much better.

Only 8,324 fans showed up at Fenway Park, the smallest Opening Day crowd since 1953, to watch us beat the Chicago White Sox 5–4. Previously I would not have been happy to see John Buzhardt on the mound starting for Chicago. Buzhardt drove me nuts my first two years with the Red Sox. He didn't throw hard, but I couldn't hit him. He'd throw me tailing fastballs in and sliders away in the dirt, and I'd chase them time and time again. He'd throw me 2-and-0 sliders for strikes, and I'd take them because I'd be looking for a fastball. But two years in the big leagues had wised me up.

I delivered an RBI single off him in my first at-bat of the season and then the next time up was looking for a slider, got it, and hit it through a fierce crosswind into the screen for a three-run homer. We stole three bases in the first six innings, and it must have warmed Dick Williams' cold, cold heart to see the way we hustled to score what turned out to be the winning run in the sixth.

Jose Tartabull beat out an infield hit and stole second. Carl Yastrzemski hit a grounder to shortstop but busted his tail up the line and forced Ron Hansen to rush his throw. He threw it away for an error as Tartabull came around to score.

The White Sox made a run at us in the late innings and had the tying and go-ahead runs in scoring position with one out in the eighth after Tommy Agee and Tom McCraw engineered a double steal. But John Wyatt fanned Ken Berry and, after falling behind on the count 3-and-1, also struck out J.C. Martin to end the threat.

But the next day we looked like the old Red Sox again as we gave away the game to the White Sox. Even when we did something right it was wrong, at least as far as the press was concerned.

We were leading 4–3 in the bottom of the eighth, and I was on third base when Williams gave our pitcher, Hank Fischer, the squeeze sign. He executed it perfectly, and now we led by two going into the ninth. It wasn't nearly enough. We committed three errors in the ninth and failed to turn two double plays, handing the White Sox five unearned runs.

On one of the potential double plays, I flipped the ball to Reggie Smith, and Tommy Agee took him right out of the play. Reggie did a 360-degree somersault in the air and landed flat on his back. I thought his back was broken. Mike Andrews had to come out to replace him, and that was pretty much the end of Reggie's career as a second baseman.

But I give him credit for trying it.

Anyway, Hansen hit one off The Wall to drive in the tying and winning runs, and we lost 8–5. There were only 3,607 fans in the stands, a normal crowd for us, but they let us have it like there were 10 times that many. It was certainly nothing we hadn't been hearing from them for years. Or from the press.

"Just as predictable as the swallows flying back to Capistrano, as certain as water seeking its own level, ineptness and vitriol have returned to Fenway Park," Ray Fitzgerald wrote in the *Boston Globe.*

Williams tried to downplay our five errors, promising the writers: "That won't happen very often." But the biggest criticism in the papers the next morning wasn't the five errors; it was the squeeze bunt.

"Inside baseball is good baseball in any park," Harold Kaese wrote in the *Globe*. "But in Fenway Park, power baseball is better. It's that kind of park, always has been."

BILLY ROHR

The first real sign that 1967 might be a special year occurred the next day in Yankee Stadium. Whitey Ford, winner of 232 regular-season games and 10 more in the World Series, was pitching for the Yankees in their home opener against Billy Rohr, a 25-year-old lefthander making his first major-league start.

Rohr was a skinny, 6'3", 170-pounder who had pitched three no-hitters in his senior year at Bellflower High School in Garden Grove, California, back in 1963. Plenty of scouts were looking at him, including Jerry Stephenson from the Red Sox, but only the Pittsburgh Pirates seemed to think he might be exceptional. They signed him for a $40,000 bonus—a lot of money in those days—and sent him to Kingsport, Tennessee, in the Appalachian League but wouldn't let him pitch.

This was still a year before the advent of baseball's amateur draft. For 15 years teams had been outbidding each other and paying huge signing bonuses to amateurs, and the spending had spiraled out of control. All sorts of rules had been passed to try to prevent the hoarding of prospects, and most of them were routinely circumvented. Because teams could only protect a certain number of these high-priced prospects, some of them were inevitably left exposed to a special draft after their first year in professional baseball. The Red Sox lost Jim Fregosi, Glenn Beckert, and Amos Otis in those drafts, but acquired Reggie Smith and Joe Foy through the same process.

In 1963 the Pirates had more such prospects than they could protect, and they stashed three pitchers at Kingsport they didn't want to risk losing. Those pitchers would work out with the team and throw batting practice, then shower and dress in their civvies and sit in the stands during the games. One of them was Billy Rohr.

Red Sox scout Mace Brown got wind of what the Pirates were up to and drove to Kingsport. "I'd like to tell you I spotted the kid pitching out back of the outfield fence or behind the grand stand. It would make me sound smart," Mace said later. "But I actually never saw the boy pitch."

But he told Neil Mahoney, the Red Sox farm director, what he had learned, and Mahoney contacted Jerry Stephenson. Stephenson reported Rohr as being "not overwhelmingly fast . . . knows how to pitch . . . good curve . . . knows how to play."

Mahoney figured that if the Pirates were going to all this trouble of trying to hide the kid, he was worth taking a gamble on.

Red Sox fans started paying attention again after Bill Rohr came within one out of throwing a no-hitter against the Yankees in his major-league debut.

So that winter the Red Sox plucked Rohr off the Pittsburgh roster for the $8,000 draft price.

Rohr began to blossom at Toronto in 1966, posting a 14–10 record with a 3.55 ERA, then pitched well enough in spring training that Williams kept him. Now he was making his major-league debut in the House that Ruth Built, going head to head with a future Hall of Fame lefthander in Whitey Ford.

Rohr wasn't the only Red Sox playing his first major-league game that day. Russ Gibson, who had toiled for 10 long years in the minors before making the big club in spring training, was going to catch him. Gibby was familiar with Rohr, having caught him in Toronto.

"I was nervous, and I knew Rohr was twice as nervous," the 27-year-old rookie catcher admitted. "My job was to not let him know it, to keep cool and relaxed out there, like Mike Ryan. That's one of Mike's wonderful qualities. It inspires confidence in a pitcher."

Rohr roomed with Jim Lonborg, and Lonnie noticed that the kid was so nervous that he tossed and turned all night and couldn't sleep. Dennis Bennett also noticed the butterflies the next day during batting practice. "If he gets by the first inning, he'll be okay," Bennett predicted. "But he's a nervous wreck right now."

Rohr was fidgety from start to finish. After every pitch he'd get the ball back from the catcher and walk around the mound. Then he'd get back on the mound and throw a pitch, and he'd be okay. When he got the ball back it started all over again, and the deeper we went into the game the worse it got.

Around the third or fourth inning we realized what was happening, and so did he even though, keeping with baseball tradition, we didn't talk about it in the dugout. Rohr hadn't allowed a hit yet. In the field we wanted to get to every ball. Not just get to it, but catch it. Gotta catch it! Keep the no-hitter going! That wasn't easy with the weather being cold and Rohr taking so much time between pitches. Fielders start to lose focus and lean back on their heels when pitchers work too slowly.

But, with a little luck and a lot of determination, we made all the plays behind him. In the sixth Bill Robinson smashed a ball up the middle that struck Rohr in the shin but caromed directly to Joe Foy at third. Foy was alert and threw Robinson out. Tom Tresh hit a drive over the head of left fielder Carl Yastrzemski leading off the ninth, a certain double until Yaz raced back and, stretching his body far beyond his 5-foot-11-inch height, somehow made a fantastic diving catch. He rolled over and held the ball aloft to show the umpires he'd caught it.

Rohr came within one strike of pitching a no-hitter. But with two outs he hung a 3-and-2 curveball to Elston Howard, who lashed it into right-center for a single. Tony Conigliaro was angry as he fielded the ball and fired it into second. We all were. We all glared at Ellie, and if looks could kill he would have been buried under first base. Rohr finished with a one-hitter, and we won 3–0.

"It was the only time in my life I got a hit in New York and got booed," Howard said. Ellie didn't know it then, but he was going to get booed again in New York after he got picked up on waivers by the Red Sox in August.

INFURIATING DICK WILLIAMS

We lost the next two games 1–0 and 7–6 in 18 innings. We blew 3–0 and 5–3 leads before tying up Sunday's game in the ninth. We had 13 at-bats with runners in scoring position in extra innings but couldn't get anyone home, and Dick Williams was livid. This was the stuff we had worked so hard to master during spring training, and it was like we had forgotten how to do it as soon as we left Florida. George Scott had four chances to win the game in extra innings and struck out in three of them, and earlier in the game he had ignored a take sign with Conigliaro on second with nobody out and swung at a 3-and-0 pitch, grounding out harmlessly to short and earning a $50 fine. Williams told the press afterward that "talking to him was like talking to cement."

We had to fly to Chicago after the game, and Williams ordered a mandatory workout for early the next afternoon. A few of us were excused, but Boomer, Joe Foy, and Jose Tartabull—who all had played the full 18 innings—were not. It was bitterly cold the next morning, so Williams canceled the workout. But he benched Boomer, who had not driven in a run in the first five games and had struck out nine times.

"I told him that if he kept striking out the way he has, it would be about 300 for the year. That would be some record," Williams said. He also ordered Boomer to lose some weight, noting he had packed on nearly 25 pounds since winning the Triple Crown in Pittsfield in 1964.

After we lost to the White Sox, Williams told the writers he was benching Foy, too, because of poor fielding. He also wanted Foy to drop ten pounds. The Red Sox had a Patriots Day doubleheader scheduled for the next morning in Boston, and when the writers asked him what his lineup was going to be, Williams cagily replied: "Get there early. It will be a lulu. The guys who play will be the guys who want to play."

The doubleheader was postponed because it was snowing, but the posted lineup had Tony Horton at first base, Mike Andrews at second, me at short, Dalton Jones at third, Yaz in left, Smith in center, Tony C. in right, and Gibson catching.

"Except for Foy, this is what I wanted to play all along in spring training," Williams proclaimed. "We have too much talent to stay ninth or tenth."

It sounded like he was trying to find another way to get the message across to George Scott. It was incomprehensible that Williams truly believed Horton was a better player than Boomer, even though Horton had produced for him in Toronto. Horton was almost as bad a first baseman as Dick Stuart had been, and while he had some offensive ability, he was wound tighter than a golf ball. Tony put incredible pressure on himself to succeed. Dick O'Connell finally traded Horton, along with Don Demeter, to Cleveland in June in exchange for pitcher Gary Bell. Horton had one real good year for the Indians, in 1969 when he hit .278 with 27 homers and 93 RBIs. But he had a breakdown shortly after that and spent some time in a mental hospital.

"There were times when I wanted to take him into a dark alley and put a licking on him," Boomer said of Williams many years later. "But the next day, you realized you were a better ballplayer than you had been the day before."

MORE ROHR

Billy Rohr faced the Yankees again on April 21, and although it was only 45 degrees and our record was 2–4, a large crowd of 25,603 turned up at Fenway Park to see the phenom. He didn't throw a no-hitter, but he didn't disappoint anyone. Instead of facing future Hall of Famer Whitey Ford this time, he was opposed by an even more formidable adversary: Mel Stottlemyre. Stottlemyre had eaten up the Red Sox ever since joining the Yankees, owning a 9–1 record against us. Mel was a real pro. He had a great sinker and a good slider. He could put the ball where he wanted, and he was tough. He had also thrown shutouts in his first two starts in 1967, including beating us 1–0 in New York.

This time we got to him and led 6–0 after seven innings. Elston Howard was again the spoiler, though, breaking up Rohr's shutout by singling home the only Yankees run in the eighth inning.

THE BENCH JOCKEY

Like I've said before, Dick Williams was a master at needling ballplayers. But he didn't limit his insults to the guys wearing uniforms. He was on the umpires all the time, and when he argued with them he used words I never knew existed! He said some real nasty things.

On April 23, in a 7–5 loss to the Yankees, Yaz got tossed in the fifth inning by veteran umpire Red Flaherty for arguing over a strike call. Williams got into it with Flaherty and was ejected, too.

After the game Williams told the press that Flaherty was "incompetent" and talked like he has "a mouthful of mush." Informed that such comments might get him in trouble with Joe Cronin, the American League president, whose offices were located at Fenway Park and who often attended Red Sox games, Williams snorted: "Maybe if he'd stayed past the fourth inning, he'd have seen how bad Flaherty was."

Well, Cal Hubbard, the AL's supervisor of umpires, stayed for the whole game, Williams was told. "Yeah," Williams sneered, "but he had his earmuffs on, so he didn't hear anything."

Williams always had it in for Flaherty. When it came to umpires, Flaherty was Williams' George Scott. He was on him all the time, and it didn't matter if he was umpiring first, second, or third base. I didn't think picking on Flaherty was a good strategy, because he'd get flustered and lose his concentration when Williams was riding him. Instead of getting better, he'd get worse. That just gave Williams even more ammunition.

Williams could have been fined by the league for his comments that day but got off with a reprimand.

A TASTE OF FIRST PLACE

In spite of our ragged start, by the end of April we found ourselves sharing first place when we beat the Kansas City Athletics 11–10 in a 15-inning game at Fenway. This was one of the many dramatic games we won in 1967 that, after the season was over and we had captured the pennant by the thin margin of a single game, you could look back on and realize just how crucial winning a game like this was.

We fell behind 5–2 in the early innings, then surged ahead 8–5. After nine the score was deadlocked 9–9. The A's had a chance to win it in the 12th, but Yaz threw out Roger Repoz trying to score from second on a single by Bert Campaneris.

In the 15th inning the A's finally seized the lead when rookie Rick Monday hit his first major-league homer off Don McMahon. Jack Aker had thrown eight innings of scoreless relief against us with eight strikeouts, and it looked like we were cooked. But we got to him.

Jose Tartabull, with his two sons, was one of many Kansas City refugees who helped us win the pennant in 1967. Four-year-old Danny (right) later became one of baseball's premier sluggers.

Tony C. led off with a single. Even though I was off to the best start of my career, batting .362 and ranking second in the league in hitting behind Detroit's Al Kaline at the time, Williams ordered me to bunt, and I sacrificed Tony to second. George Scott, back in the manager's good graces for the moment, singled, but Conigliaro had to hold up at third. Dalton Jones pinch hit for Russ Gibson and walked, loading the bases.

Williams sent up Jose Tartabull to pinch hit for Mike Andrews, and he slapped a single between first and second, bringing home Tony and Boomer to win the game.

And all of a sudden we found ourselves in a tie for first place with the Yankees.

We didn't stay there long. The next afternoon a crowd of 31,450 crammed its way into Fenway Park, the club's first sellout since Opening Day in 1960. It was Bat Day, and the Red Sox gave away 18,000 bats to the kids. They must have included our bats by mistake, because we got only five hits off Jim Nash and lost 1–0 when Danny Cater hit a homer off Darrell Brandon in the second inning. We dropped into third place with an 8–6 record, one game behind first-place Detroit and a half-game behind the Yankees.

4

MAY 1967

It wasn't exactly the merry, merry month of May for us, at least not at the beginning. We started the month on the West Coast, where Dennis Bennett not only shut out the California Angels 4–0 but provided most of the offense by belting a three-run homer. George Scott also connected for his first homer of the year.

But we lost eight of the next ten games and saw our record plunge to 11–14, putting us in a tie for eighth place, 6 ½ games behind the Detroit Tigers, who were off to a 17–7 start. No one outside of us was surprised to see us that low in the standings. But we had some unexpected company in eighth place. The two most recent American League champions, the defending world champion Baltimore Orioles and Minnesota Twins, were right there with us.

THE EMERGENCE OF GENTLEMAN JIM

If there was a silver lining to those dark days in the first three weeks of May, it was the pitching of Jim Lonborg. Lonnie was already off to a good start, going 2–0 in April with a 3.46 ERA

Jim Lonborg, under the tutelage of pitching coach Sal "The Barber" Maglie, learned how to intimidate hitters by 1967 and won 22 games and the Cy Young Award. (*Courtesy of the Boston Red Sox*)

and 26 strikeouts in 25 ⅔ innings. But it was a tough 2–1 loss to the Angels in Anaheim on May 3 that grabbed the attention of our opponents and proved he had arrived as a major-league ace.

Lonnie had never beaten the Angels in 11 tries, and he wasn't going to beat them this time, either. But that night he retired the first 17 Angels in order and took a no-hitter into the seventh inning. He was working on a one-hitter in the ninth and fiercely protecting a 1–0 lead—courtesy of a Mike Andrews homer in the fifth inning—when Jim Fregosi, Jay Johnstone, and Rick Reichardt stroked one-out singles to tie the game. After getting the second out, Lonnie bounced a pitch that Russ Gibson blocked and kept in front of him. But Gibby thought it was behind him, and while he was looking around for the ball Lonnie dashed in to try to get it. Johnstone outraced him to the plate and scored the winning run.

After the game the Angels had nothing but praise for Lonborg's performance.

"He had the best stuff I've ever seen him have," Fregosi said.

"Lonborg's the most impressive pitcher we've seen this year," Reichardt added.

"That kid is going to be something," said Angels manager Bill Rigney. "He's learning how to be a pitcher now, and he has the arm to go with it. His fastball moves the way Dick Radatz's pitch used to when he was going good, and there wasn't a tougher pitch to hit than that."

Lonnie's confidence just kept growing during 1967. He always had the ability. He had a great tail on his fastball. It moved about a foot. He could throw it at the middle of the plate, and it would tail right in on right-handed hitters, get right in their kitchen, as the saying goes. He also had a curveball he threw right at right-handed hitters, and their knees would buckle before it broke. Lonborg was intimidating, but he wasn't mean, not like his pitching coach, Sal Maglie, had been. Yeah, Lonnie led the league in hit batsmen in 1967. But a lot of the guys he hit that year he didn't hit on purpose. He would when the situation dictated it, though. He wasn't afraid to knock somebody on his rear end.

A TWIN KILLING

The next stop on the road trip was Minnesota, where our record was pathetic. From 1964–66, the Red Sox had lost 27 of their 30 games at Metropolitan Stadium. If the Twins appeared beatable in 1967, you couldn't prove it by us. We lost the first two games and were on the verge of being swept.

Carl Yastrzemski, the highest-paid player on the team with a salary of $58,000, was mired in a 4-for-32 slump with no RBIs, and Dick Williams benched him in the last game of the series against southpaw Jim Kaat. "I don't care how much they're earning. I'm trying to win ballgames," Williams said. "Yaz wasn't hitting righties, so how was he going to hit a lefty?"

To Yaz's credit, he didn't put up a fuss. "I didn't mind," he told the press. "It gave me a chance to collect my thoughts."

We found ourselves down 5–1 after three innings. But a two-run pinch double by Tony Horton tied the game up at 5–5, and in the seventh George Scott coaxed a two-out walk from Jim Perry and Don Demeter doubled. I had struck out in each of my first three at-bats, but this time I dumped a single into left, scoring Boomer and Demeter and putting us ahead 7–5. A throwing error by third baseman Ron Clark gave us two more runs in the inning, and we hung on to win 9–6.

The first two Twins reached in the ninth against Dan Osinski, and we started getting nervous. Were we going to find a way to lose again at the Met? But John Wyatt ambled in from the bullpen and nailed down the save, his first of the season. He struck out a pair of future Hall of Famers, Rod Carew and Harmon Killebrew, sandwiched around a walk to Zoilo Versalles that loaded the bases, then retired slugger Bob Allison on a grounder to end the game.

Wyatt was off to a terrific start for us. He had pitched 15 ⅓ innings and had yet to allow a run. He had given up only six hits and had struck out 14 batters.

JOHN WYATT

To this day John Wyatt is remembered best by Red Sox fans for getting hit in the back of the head by a throw from catcher Bob Tillman, who was trying to cut down a runner stealing second base. That's unfair, because we couldn't have won the pennant without him.

After Dick Radatz flamed out and was traded to Cleveland for pitchers Don McMahon and Lee Stange on June 2, 1966, the Red Sox needed somebody reliable to come out of the bullpen and pitch the final innings of close games. Less than two weeks after trading Radatz, general manager Dick O'Connell acquired the 31-year-old Wyatt, along with Jose Tartabull, from the Kansas City Athletics in exchange for outfielder Jim Gosger and pitchers Ken Sanders and Guido Grilli. It turned out to be a heckuva deal for us.

Wyatt had originally been signed by the St. Louis Cardinals and had posted a decent 12–11 record in Class D ball his first year. He expected a promotion the next year and instead got released during spring training.

"You know how they do that?" he recalled with bitterness.

"They don't tell you or nothin'. You come to the park one day and your uniform ain't in your locker. You figure it out."

The Cardinals didn't think Wyatt threw hard enough to pitch in the majors.

By the mid-1950s the Negro Leagues had begun to disband now that the major leagues had accepted integration, and one of the few remaining clubs was the Indianapolis Clowns, who barnstormed around the country. The Black Yankees were their foils, like the Washington Generals were to the Harlem Globetrotters in basketball. The two teams played games in as many as three cities a day. The Black Yankees were supposed to be competitive, but they weren't supposed to win. After getting released by the Cardinals, Wyatt signed a contract with the Black Yankees for $200 a month.

"The Yankees traveled in this old yellow school bus with straight-back seats," Wyatt recalled. "The Clowns had this big modern bus with reclining seats. Everyone on the Yankees wanted to get on the Clowns."

John Wyatt anchored our bullpen in 1967, saving 20 games and winning 10 more. (*Courtesy of the Boston Red Sox*)

Wyatt did after beating the Clowns three straight times. But he wasn't making enough money to eat, and after losing 30 pounds he asked for his release and received it. Wyatt returned to Buffalo, New York, where he had grown up, and was pitching semipro ball when he was spotted by a scout for the Kansas City Athletics and was signed to a contract.

Wyatt worked his way through the minors until reaching the majors in 1961. Wyatt pitched very well, albeit in obscurity, for a bad Athletics team for four years, saving 20 or more games twice for the A's in an era when complete games were far more common and a 20-save season was the standard of excellence. In 1964 Wyatt led AL pitchers with 81 appearances and won or saved more than half the Athletics' 57 victories that year. But when he got off to a rough start in 1966, the Athletics deemed him expendable and traded him to us. He pitched fine for the Red Sox the rest of the way, going 3–4 with eight saves and a 3.14 ERA in 42 games.

The scuttlebutt around baseball was that Wyatt threw a spitter, applying Vaseline to the ball. It wasn't a rumor. He called his favorite pitch the "wazleen ball," and it was a real greaser. There was always a jar of Vaseline visible on the shelf in his locker. He didn't try to hide it. Maybe, like Gaylord Perry later on when he came over to the American League, Wyatt was shrewd enough to know the spitter was just as effective when it was a psychological weapon. If panicked hitters were so focused on looking for it, he didn't even have to throw it. He could get them out with a different pitch. Perry had a routine of touching different parts of his uniform before throwing a pitch, and hitters were convinced he was getting the substance he was using, K-Y jelly, from one of those spots to load up the ball. His routine would drive the hitters wild, especially when the umpires could never find anything when they checked him.

I don't know where Perry hid it, but Wyatt did have Vaseline all over his uniform. "John, you getting it?" we'd ask him before games. "Yeah, I'm gettin' it," he'd say. He put different amounts in different spots, and depending on how much he needed he'd go to the bill of his cap or behind his head or under his belt. Under his belt was where he kept "The Blob," the biggest cache of goo. Almost every pitch he threw was loaded.

Wyatt saved 20 games for the Red Sox in 1967, tying him with Chicago's Bob Locker for second in the league in that department, and won 10 more. The only relief pitcher who won or saved more games than Wyatt that year was California's Minnie Rojas, who had 12 wins and 27 saves.

Five days after that save against the Twins, Wyatt got beaned by Tillman in a game against the Detroit Tigers at Fenway Park. Al Kaline drew a walk off Wyatt and attempted to steal second base. I was covering second on the play, and I saw Tillman throw, and then I was wondering what happened to the ball. It just disappeared. Wyatt turned around to watch the play and forgot to duck, and Tillman's throw hit him squarely in the back of the head. Wyatt went down, and ball ended up in the on-deck circle between home and first base as Kaline went around to third. Wyatt stayed in and finished the game, though, and Kaline scored on a sacrifice fly moments later, giving the Tigers a 5–2 lead.

"I threw the heck out of it," Tillman said. "I think it would have been right on target. It was probably the best throw I made all year."

Unfortunately, that run proved to be the difference in the game. We scored two runs in the bottom of the ninth but fell short, losing 5–4.

I don't know if Williams blamed Tillman more than Wyatt, but Tillman didn't start another game for 38 days and got into only four games in the interim. Tillman had been with the Red Sox since 1962 and their regular catcher until 1966, but Williams didn't like him much as a player. I think he kept him around in case the inexperienced catchers, Mike Ryan and Russ Gibson, couldn't handle the job or got hurt. A few days after we picked up

Elston Howard from the Yankees in early August, Dick O'Connell sold Tillman to the Yankees.

THE EVOLUTION OF YAZ

I don't know whether or not Wyatt might have been battling the effects of that beaning—nobody knew much about concussions in those days—but the next day was his worst day of the season for us. We handed him a 5–4 lead to protect, and for 1 ⅔ innings he did. But the Tigers shelled him for six runs in the top of the ninth, and we lost 10–8.

That was the last loss in that brutal 10-game stretch. The next day we swept a doubleheader from the Tigers and knocked them out of first place while jumping five places in the standings ourselves into a tie for third. Both games were slugfests as 12 homers were hit, six by each team.

I belted a pair of homers in the first game, which we won 8–5. I had a single and a double in the second game, which we won 13–9, and finished the afternoon with five runs batted in and four runs scored. I was off to the best start of my major-league career, hitting .320 and ranking among the league leaders in batting.

That was also the day Carl Yastrzemski, who had hit as many as 20 homers just once in his first six seasons, began to blossom as a power hitter. The first two years I had been with the Red Sox, most of the home runs I saw Yaz hit were to left or left-center. He didn't pull the ball much. Now his off-season strength regimen and tinkering with his stance in spring training started to pay dividends. Yaz also asked our hitting coach, Bobby Doerr—whose 223 homers ranked second to Ted Williams on the Red Sox' all-time home run list at the time—for some tips. A few hours before the doubleheader, Doerr worked with Yaz and noticed his hands were too low when he cocked his bat.

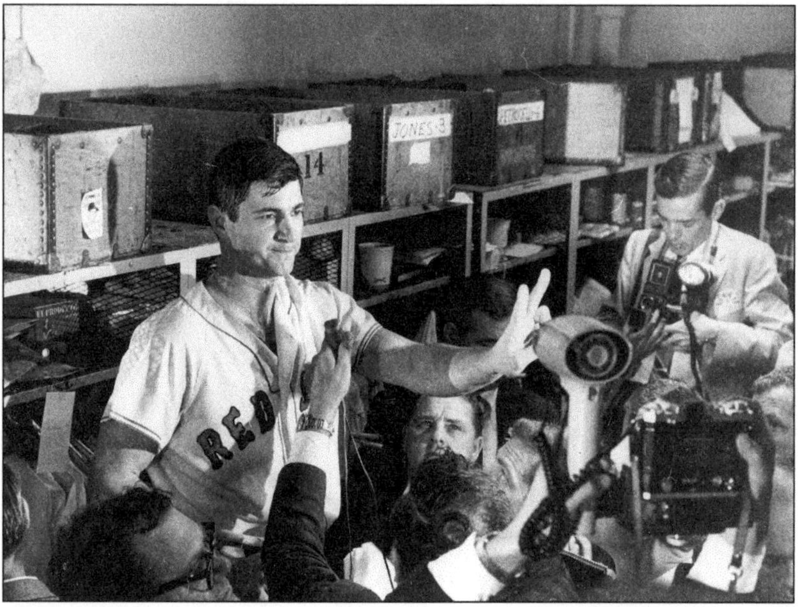

Even in the clubhouse, Carl Yastrzemski stood above the crowd during his incredible Triple Crown season in 1967. (*Courtesy of the Boston Red Sox*)

"We discussed it a bit, and Carl felt we were on to something," Doerr wrote in the diary he kept during the 1967 season. "When he got back in, he held his hands higher, about to the level of his left ear. He started hitting the ball all over, with power. By raising his bat, he leveled his swing and the ball carried with good backspin. Up to now, with his hands dropped, he's been hitting with an uppercut, causing an overspin on the ball. A lot of potential home runs were sinking and dying in the outfield."

Yaz, who had hit only two homers in the first month of the season, socked one in each game of the doubleheader and five in a four-game stretch. After watching Yaz belt a pair of homers in a 12–8 loss to the Baltimore Orioles on May 17, George Scott commented: "That guy is gonna have some kind of year!" Nostradamus couldn't have said it any better.

THE GIFT OF HARD WORK

Everyone was surprised when Yaz started hitting all those homers in 1967. He had never hit very many before then—95 in his first six seasons, to be exact, an average of less than 16 a year. I read the papers every day, and what was written about Yaz was unfair most of the time. Sure, he had his bad games. Everybody does. But with Yaz the expectations were insanely high. Everybody was hoping he'd be the next Ted Williams, and the pressure was on him to carry on the tradition. Eventually he did, of course, but not in the early sixties. When he didn't start off his career by hitting 31 homers the way Ted did—Yaz hit only 11 in his rookie year—a lot of Red Sox fans were disappointed.

Yaz had a lot of respect for Williams. But he never tried to be Williams. There was only one Ted Williams, and Yaz just wanted to be Yaz. But I know he felt he should have done a lot better than he did in the early years, although the fact that those teams he played on weren't very good made it frustrating for everybody, including Carl.

Baseball didn't come as naturally to Yaz as a lot of people think. He had to work at it, and he did so for hours. He'd take extra batting practice after night games and come in on off-days to hit. He also worked very hard on his fielding, learning to charge balls hard so he could throw out runners at home. And he played The Wall great! Winning all those Gold Gloves in left field didn't just happen; he had to work at it.

His powers of concentration were immense. He never let the criticism get to him the way Ted Williams sometimes had. Yaz was mentally tough and could leave whatever happened off the field behind him and just concentrate on the game.

A SONG FOR THE SOX

While we were starting to hit the ball hard as a team, our opponents were hitting it even harder in mid-May. In one span of six games, our pitchers were mauled for 56 runs and surrendered a staggering total of 17 homers in the last 37 innings of that stretch, including seven to the Orioles—four of them in one inning—in that 12–8 defeat.

That prompted the *Boston Globe's* Ray Fitzgerald, one of the wittiest baseball writers around, to pen the following ditty, sung to the tune of "Take Me Out to the Ball Game."

Take me out of the ball game,
Get me out of this mess.
Drag me away from the fence so green.
Don't make me look at the left-field screen.
Oh, it's fun, fun, fun for the other guys,
But for me it's strictly a shame.
When Brooks and Frank and everyone else
Hits them out at the old ball game.

Dick Williams was just as fed up as the press and the fans. He stuck Billy Rohr, who hadn't won since pitching those two gems against the Yankees, in the bullpen and inserted Jose Santiago into the rotation. Santiago would respond by going 12–4 for us, but nobody knew that then.

"We're pretty close to bringing somebody up from Toronto," Williams told the writers. Jerry Stephenson and Gary Waslewski were both off to impressive starts for the Maple Leafs, and Dave Morehead seemed to have recovered from his arm problems and was striking out a lot of guys. "We might as well get young guys who can throw hard. We don't seem to be getting anybody out this way."

While the pitching staff was getting lit up, Williams got off the backs of the position players for a while and devoted his energies to chewing out the pitchers. As hard as he could be on us, Williams was always toughest on the pitchers. Man, he was really rough on them! I remember one time later in the season when he went out to the mound and called Waslewski every name in the book. If he'd ever said the things to me he said to Waslewski, I'd have punched him in the mouth right there! I was just standing there with my mouth open and thinking: "I can't believe he just said that!" And Waslewski just stood there and took it.

Jim Lonborg made it 18 homers in 38 innings on May 19 when Cleveland's Leon Wagner hit a pop fly that barely reached the nets for a patented Fenway Park two-run homer in the first inning.

"Here we go again. That's all I could think," Lonnie moaned.

But he gave up only three more hits after that and fanned 12 batters, his second double-digit strikeout game of the young season. A slimmed-down Joe Foy hit a homer for us in the seventh off Gary Bell, but we were still losing 2–1 going into the bottom of the ninth.

Jose Tartabull pinch hit for Mike Ryan and beat out a chopper over the mound. Dalton Jones pinch hit for Lonnie and sacrificed. Reggie Smith then belted a triple off the center-field wall to tie the game, finishing Bell. Tony Horton pinch hit for Mike Andrews and greeted reliever Orlando Pena with a single to right field that brought in Reggie with the winning run. Tony was so excited he almost forgot to run to first base.

That 3–2 victory straightened out our pitching. Starting with that game, we would give up more than three runs in a game just six times in a 17-game stretch and win 11 times.

A DIFFERENT UNIFORM

We managed to win without Tony Conigliaro during that period. The war in Vietnam was beginning to escalate, and to avoid being drafted, a lot of young ballplayers were joining the Army Reserve. Tony had joined after the 1965 season and spent the next six months in basic training at Fort Dix, New Jersey. Reservists were required to attend regular meetings and also go on active duty for two weeks each year. Tony's unit was sent to Camp Drum, New York, from May 19 until June 3. Tony was hitting .304 with a couple of homers and 15 RBIs in 23 games for us at the time, and his bat would be missed.

Every major-league team lost some players to reserve duty during those years. But because the Red Sox were the youngest team in the league, I think those absences worked more of a hardship on us than any other club.

In addition to Tony C., Jim Lonborg, Mike Andrews, Dalton Jones, Billy Rohr, Bill Landis, and I were also serving in the reserves.

In fact, Lonnie and I were nearly sent to Vietnam. The Red Sox got us into an Army Reserve unit while we were playing in Seattle in 1964, and we took our basic training at Fort Leonard Wood in Missouri after the season. Right at the end of basic we were told our unit was being activated and sent to Vietnam. Our gear was all packed, and we were ready to go. At the last minute, they told us it was called off. Whew!

THE COMEBACK KIDS

We showed a lot of spunk during that Cleveland series. The Indians took a 3–0 lead into the seventh inning the next day before we tied up the game on a two-run double by Dalton Jones and a single by me. The Indians finally beat us in the 10th when Chuck Hinton hit a two-run homer off Don McMahon.

In the first game of a doubleheader on Sunday, May 21, we found ourselves trailing Sonny Siebert, Cleveland's best pitcher, 3–0 in the eighth inning. Carl Yastrzemski hit a two-run triple to the deepest part of Fenway Park, George Scott followed with a home run, and we won 4–3. We breezed in the nightcap, winning 6–2 and getting back within a game of .500 while holding onto fourth place, 5 ½ games behind the Chicago White Sox.

"We proved we don't quit," Dick Williams declared. "We proved we can come back."

For once, the "carnivorous Boston press," as Johnny Pesky liked to call the writers, only half in jest, wasn't being negative. But the media wasn't jumping on our bandwagon just yet.

Wrote the *Boston Globe*'s Harold Kaese: "If they are only one game under .500 when the season ends, Boston rooters will rejoice; and if they are in fourth place, Dick Williams may be voted Manager of the Year."

A few days later one of the Boston newspapers polled the players, asking which team they thought would win the pennant. We were instructed not to vote for ourselves. I guess the paper didn't want what could be perceived as phony rah-rah quotes from a team that hadn't won a pennant in 20 years or enjoyed a winning season in eight mucking up what was supposed to be a serious analysis. Regardless of how strongly we felt about our own chances, most of us heeded the instructions. Baltimore, the defending world champs, and Detroit were the consensus picks, although I threw the Twins into the mix. How could I not? The Twins looked like world champs every time we'd played them since I'd come up to the big leagues.

Yaz, however, couldn't resist casting a vote for us. "Why not?" he argued. "The Tigers, Orioles, and White Sox are the top ones, but I'd put us up there, too. Nobody's going to run away with it this season."

He was right. Four teams went into the final four days of the season separated by just 1 ½ games. And the Red Sox would be one of them.

LONBORG MAKES A TRANSITION

We embarked on a six-game road trip that would be a real test for us: three games in Detroit against the second-place Tigers, who were 21–11; and three in Baltimore against the Orioles, who were playing well again after a slow start and were only .001 behind us in the standings.

We got off to a terrific start on the trip. Carl Yastrzemski and I both clouted homers, and we beat the Tigers 5–2 in the first game. Jim Lonborg shut out the Tigers 1–0 the next night, beating Denny McLain, who was destined to become a 31-game winner a year later. Lonnie pitched a four-hitter and struck out 11, but he also walked four and seemed to be in some kind of trouble every inning. Three times the Tigers had a runner on third with less than two outs and failed to score.

"I have thrown better games, but I have never pitched a better game," Lonnie said afterward, emphasizing the subtle difference between being a thrower and a pitcher. "I got tough men out when it meant something."

With runners at first and third in the second inning, Lonnie struck out Bill Freehan and got Ray Oyler to bounce into a double play. The Tigers loaded the bases with one out in the seventh, and with the one-run lead Dick Williams decided to play it safe and had the infield playing back, conceding the tying run while praying for another double play. The problem was that the batter, Dick McAuliffe, didn't hit into very many double plays. In fact, he would ground into just two all year. The second one would come on the very last play of the regular season, sealing an 8–5 defeat at the hands of the California Angels that would give us the pennant.

As I mentioned earlier, George Scott was one of the greatest instinctive ballplayers I ever played with. McAuliffe hit the ball sharply down to Boomer, who was playing deep at first. The logical play was to throw to second and try to start that inning-ending double play we desperately wanted. But Boomer sensed we might not be able to turn it and, knowing the Tigers had a plodding runner on third in Norm Cash, elected to make the long throw to the plate to prevent the tying run from scoring. His throw was accurate and in time to get the force, and Lonnie ended the threat by getting Don Wert to foul out.

Lonborg got right back into another jam in the eighth. Al Kaline reached third with one out and seemingly scored when Jim Northrup swung and missed at a low pitch that got away from Mike Ryan. Only it wasn't a wild pitch; the ball had hit Northrup in the foot. Because he swung at it he wasn't awarded first base, but the ball was dead, and umpire Cal Drummond ordered Kaline back to third.

Lonnie fanned Northrup for the second out but now had to retire Cash. While delivering a 2-and-1 pitch, he flinched, and Williams and trainer Buddy LeRoux came rushing out of the dugout.

"Something snapped in my shoulder, and I was worried," Lonnie explained later. "But I was allowed to throw a test pitch, and I guess it went back into place."

Nowadays, no manager would dare leave a pitcher in after something like that, especially when that pitcher was his ace. But things were different then. Lonnie said he was okay, and Williams took him at his word. Lonnie had been a pre-med student at Stanford, so maybe Williams figured his pitcher knew more about anatomy than a baseball lifer did.

Cash fouled off four pitches in a row before Lonborg struck him out with a curveball.

We scored our only run because Williams decided to play Dalton Jones, our utility infielder, at third base instead of Joe Foy. In his first at-bat in the second inning Jones hit a McLain pitch into the right-field stands for a homer. Of Dalton's 17 career homers to that point, five had been hit in Tiger Stadium.

Dick Williams didn't play hunches. He knew that Jones always hit well in Detroit, and this was in an era when managers didn't have reams of statistics to pore over. I had never played for a manager as well prepared as Williams was. It takes a lot to be a good manager, more than just coming to the ballpark and making out the lineup card. The manager has to stay on top of every aspect of the game and on top of the individuals. Williams was always thinking several innings ahead. He'd tell a guy to be ready to pinch hit in the eighth inning, and that's exactly when he'd use him. After a while the guys on the bench learned to think right along with him and would start getting prepared for their roles before Williams even approached them. In that era you always expected your starting pitcher to go seven or eight innings and often nine. But sometimes a pitcher would get the stuffing kicked out of him in the second inning. Williams was always prepared for that eventuality and knew whom he was going to bring in when that happened. Williams was a manager ahead of his time.

THE ROOKIES MAKE AN IMPACT

The remainder of the road trip was a near-bust. We lost the last game in Detroit and the first two in Baltimore. The second loss to the Orioles was ugly. Frank Robinson, the reigning AL MVP and Triple Crown winner, continued to tattoo our pitching staff by belting a pair of homers to take over the league lead with 12—four of them against us—and we got smeared 10–0. We didn't help our own cause by committing six errors and wasting 10 hits. F. Robbie hit another one out the next day, but we held on for a 4–3 win and completed a 3–3 trip.

The real significance of that trip was that two of our rookies, second baseman Mike Andrews and center fielder Reggie Smith, began to contribute to the offense.

Andrews went 11-for-23 on the trip, upping his batting average to .301 and cracking the league's Top Ten. He had also laid down eight sacrifice bunts by then and didn't object to playing the game the way Dick Williams wanted it played.

"Bunting is a matter of concentrating," Andrews explained. "Sometimes it's harder than hitting, because you have to make contact. You can't be fiddling around in the batter's box."

After angering Williams in spring training by showing up hurt from an off-season weight-lifting program, Andrews was now back in the manager's good graces.

"I think I might not have been in the best of shape the first month," Andrews admitted. "When I hurt my back in spring training, I couldn't do any running, and that didn't help."

Mike Andrews had been a star shortstop at South High School in Torrance, California, and in American Legion ball. But it looked like he was going to be a tough sign because he had a scholarship offer from UCLA to play football as a split end.

"Michael's father was a halfback at the University of Montana, and I think football runs in the family," his mother told Red Sox scout Jerry Stephenson.

Stephenson (the father of the Red Sox pitcher of the same name) tried to convince her otherwise. "Michael will make more money this way, and he won't get broken bones or cracked in the head," he told her. He asked to speak to her husband, who wasn't home. He was at work, she said, running a tavern in Hermosa Beach called Callahan's.

"I eat there all the time!" Stephenson exclaimed. "Your husband's name isn't Lloyd Andrews, is it?"

It was. Stephenson hopped in his car, drove to Callahan's, talked to Lloyd Andrews, and got his son's name on a Red Sox contract. That was in 1962. Four years later Mike, by then converted into a second baseman, was in the major leagues and helping the Red Sox win a pennant.

Rookie second baseman Mike Andrews did whatever it took to win, putting down sacrifice bunts and hitting game-winning home runs. (*Courtesy of the Boston Red Sox*)

Smith was scuffling with a .191 batting average before going 10-for-26 on the trip. But Reggie and his wife, Ernestine, were going through a sad time that spring. They were trying to start a family, and for the second time a child had been born to them prematurely and had died. Reggie put up a brave front, but the loss of another baby was devastating to them. Dick Williams, for all his gruffness, was good at handling those personal situations, too, consoling guys who had a death in the family or troubles at home.

Reggie was a sensitive guy, and Williams knew that. He would get on some guys unmercifully, and he was particularly harsh on George Scott and some of the pitchers. But certain guys—like me, Reggie, and Yaz—he pretty much left alone. Williams knew which players he could push hard and which ones he shouldn't. That didn't mean the three of us got a free pass when we messed up. We'd still get a lecture. If Yaz did something wrong—which wasn't very often—Williams would take him to task, even if it was only to say: "You shouldn't have done that. You're too good a player to make a mistake like that."

Fortunately, all of us were ready for a manager like that. We were so tired of losing that when Dick Williams took over and said—or screamed—you've got to do this and you've got to do that, we believed him. And everything came together for the Red Sox in 1967. The right team and the right manager, both in the right place at the right time.

TURNING THE CORNER

We could still play ugly games from time to time, but because we were starting to do the things that Dick Williams wanted us to do, we were making fewer mistakes. In previous years we'd lose five in a row, win one, and then lose four more. Now we were avoiding those long losing streaks, and when we won, we usually kept winning for a while.

We finished the month of May riding a four-game winning streak, making us hotter than the weather. It had been the coldest May in 50 years, averaging seven degrees below normal, and temperatures had been below normal on 28 of the month's 31 days. It had also been the second-wettest May in 99 years. But Memorial Day turned out to be gorgeous, and a sellout crowd of 32,012—the largest to see a Red Sox game at Fenway Park in five years—turned up to watch us sweep a doubleheader from the ninth-place California Angels. By now attendance was up about 65,000 over the previous season. Red Sox fans were starting to get a little excited again. It was gratifying to be playing in front of people who were cheering for us and wanted us to do well. The adrenaline flowed, and we'd get pumped up.

We treated them to what was becoming a familiar and successful pattern in the first game. The Angels jumped out to a 4–0 lead and chased Jose Santiago after just three innings. Lee Stange, one of our most reliable pitchers in 1966 but who had been bothered by a sore shoulder in spring training, found his groove again and struck out seven batters over the next three scoreless innings until we rallied in the sixth.

Andrews doubled in the first run, and a bases-loaded walk to George Scott forced home another before we picked up two more runs on an error and tied the game at 4–4. In the eighth Reggie Smith walked, stole second, and scored the winning run on a pinch double by Tony Horton.

The 5–4 victory squared our record at 20–20. We would never fall under .500 again during the remainder of the 1967 season. We won the second game 6–1 and finished the month by edging our old nemesis, the Twins, 3–2.

We scored our three runs by employing what was to become our patented offense that summer under Dick Williams. Yaz would supply the long ball, and the rest of us would produce runs by playing small ball.

Yaz clubbed a pair of solo homers off Jim Perry to give us a 2–0 lead, and then in the sixth Boomer beat out an infield hit and Smith walked. Although I was fourth in the league in batting with a .325 average and second on the team with six homers and 24 RBIs, Williams ordered me to sacrifice. I bunted the runners over, and after Joe Foy was intentionally walked to load the bases, Mike Ryan neatly executed a suicide squeeze.

Although I hit some home runs, I didn't consider myself a power hitter at that point in my career. I had always been a pretty good bunter, so I was never surprised when I got the sign to sacrifice. You did what you had to do to win a game, and I always felt good about getting a bunt down and moving a couple runners over.

The important thing was that Dick Williams was still doing the things he told us in spring training we would be doing, and we did those things all summer. If a manager promises to do something one way in spring training and then doesn't follow through and do it that way during the season, he loses his credibility. If a manager says we're going to bunt and hit and run, and then when the situation comes up he doesn't do them, what does that say about him?

Billy Rohr was supposed to start for us that day but had been summoned for duty by his Army Reserve unit. Darrell Brandon filled in and should have pitched a shutout. But in the eighth I booted a double-play ball for an error that handed the Twins two unearned runs and nearly cost us the game.

Yaz made a pretty running catch on a fly by Harmon Killebrew but then made a high throw to the plate that allowed the second run to score. John Wyatt, who had relieved Brandon, was backing up the play but stumbled and fell down as the ball got away from him. Cesar Tovar, who had reached on my error, saw an opportunity to score the tying run from second base and ran hard to the plate. Wyatt recovered the ball in the nick of time and heaved it to Ryan, who tagged out Tovar and was rewarded with a couple of spike wounds on his arm.

We ended the month in third place with a 22–20 record, 4 ½ games behind the Tigers and the White Sox.

But Wyatt liked to remind us whenever we got too cocky: "There's a lot of cotton to be picked yet."

5

JUNE 1967

Our four-game winning streak came to an end on June 1 when Minnesota's Dean Chance shut us out 4–0, allowing only four hits and striking out 10. There was no shame in that; Chance was one of the best pitchers in the league. But Jim Lonborg was even more brilliant the following night against Cleveland. For the third time in the young 1967 season, Lonnie flirted with a no-hitter, taking one into the eighth inning before Duke Sims broke it up with a one-out, ground-rule double. Carl Yastrzemski continued his power surge, walloping a two-run homer in the sixth that provided Lonnie with the runs he needed to beat the Indians 2–1. Lonnie, who outpitched Sonny Siebert, had now won five in a row and was 7–1 on the season with a 2.85 ERA.

ACQUISITIONS

We raised our record to 24–21 on June 3 by beating the Indians 6–2. What was more important was we added two players that day, a familiar one and a new one. Tony Conigliaro returned from his two weeks of Army duty and went right into the lineup. He looked rusty, going hitless and striking out in two of his three at-bats.

Utility infielder Jerry Adair was quiet off the field, but he sure made a lot of noise on it. We couldn't have won the pennant without him. (*Courtesy of the Boston Red Sox*)

Dick O'Connell, the general manager, swapped reliever Don McMahon and a minor-league pitcher named Rob Snow to the Chicago White Sox in exchange for utility infielder Jerry Adair. This would turn out to be a fabulous deal for us. We knew he'd had some good years with Baltimore, and we knew he was a terrific fielder. What we didn't realize right away was how much of a spark plug the versatile Adair was going to be for us. Next to Yaz and Lonborg, he would be the best clutch player we had. The big hits he got for us to keep rallies going, tie games, and win games were almost too many to count. It seemed like Adair was part of every big game we won.

Adair was a taciturn man. He never said very much. He just went out and did the job he was paid to do and did it extremely well. Jerry's contribution to a brief conversation was "Hi." His contribution to a lengthy conversation was "Hello."

Adair's arrival also gave Dick Williams a suitable backup for me at shortstop. I had played nearly every game so far, more games than anybody else on the club, partly because I was hitting and doing the things the manager wanted me to do and partly because Williams didn't have much faith in anyone else to play shortstop. Adair would fill in admirably for me after I got hurt later in the month.

Adair had long been a favorite of Red Sox scout Danny Doyle, who had courted him through high school and then college at Oklahoma A&M (now Oklahoma State University). Doyle had never put any pressure on Adair to sign, respecting his desire to get an education, and his patience wound up costing the Sox a good player when Adair decided to skip his senior year of college and sign a contract with the Baltimore Orioles in 1958.

"Though I had been close to him for five years or more, the Red Sox had never actually talked contract with me," Adair explained later. "I guess Dan took it for granted I'd go back for my final year of college."

Adair went straight from the campus to Baltimore, and by 1961 he had become a regular on those strong Orioles clubs. He set major-league records by playing 89 consecutive games and handling 458 chances without an error at second base in Baltimore. The Orioles dealt him to the White Sox in 1966, and now he was finally a Red Sox.

The next day O'Connell swung another trade, this one with the Indians for 30-year-old pitcher Gary Bell, whom we had already beaten twice in 1967, including the previous day. Bell had been a pretty good pitcher for the Indians, notably in 1959 when he went 16–11. By the mid-1960s the Indians had become a mediocre team. Bell, who had been a reliever for several seasons, went back into the rotation in 1966 and pitched better than his 14–15 record indicated. In fact, he made the All-Star team for the second time in his career. His ERA was 3.22, and in 254 innings he had allowed only 211 hits and registered a career-high 194 strikeouts, fifth-best in the league. He was a hard thrower who was hard to hit.

But in 1967 Bell was just another pitcher on a hard-throwing staff that included "Sudden" Sam McDowell, Luis Tiant, and Sonny Siebert. A good day against those guys was when you went 0-for-4 and didn't strike out three times. Off to a 1–5 start, Bell became expendable, and the Indians were desperate for some offense. So they traded Bell to the Red Sox for Tony Horton.

We wouldn't miss Horton's mitt. We were sorry to lose his bat. He wasn't playing much, but he was 6-for-13 as a pinch hitter for us with two game-winning hits. George Scott was probably the happiest man on the team to see Horton depart. He knew first base now belonged exclusively to him.

Bell would stabilize our rotation and go 12–8 with a 3.16 ERA after joining us. He won five games in June alone, and that was a big lift. Unlike Adair, who wasn't one for long conversations, Gary was a true character. He had a wonderful sense of humor, made fun of everybody, and helped keep the clubhouse loose.

STANKY SPEAKS AND YAZ WREAKS HAVOC

Carl Yastrzemski was a prankster who kept the clubhouse loose, too. And vigilant. One of his favorite practical jokes was to crawl under the seats of the team bus and give someone a hotfoot. You wouldn't know what he was doing until your toes started to burn up. A few years later we nicknamed him "The Slasher." When the Red Sox acquired Luis Aparicio in 1971 Yaz found the perfect foil for his pranks. He constantly shredded Aparicio's ties, pants, and suits. He did the same thing to pitcher Ken Tatum.

Otherwise Yaz—especially to outsiders—was a relatively emotionless guy who went about his business in a professional manner. But, like Baltimore's Frank Robinson, Yaz wasn't someone you wanted to get riled up. If a pitcher knocked him down, Yaz would quickly make him regret it. Some pitchers were slow learners, though. Take Detroit's Mickey Lolich, for example. Every time Lolich faced Yaz, he'd knock him down. And Yaz would get right back up and get a hit off him. Lolich never learned.

White Sox manager Eddie Stanky, who had played for the Boston Braves in 1948 when they won the National League pennant, and Dick Williams were a lot alike. They had both stuck around for a long time as players because they would stop at nothing to win, and they were both accomplished bench jockeys. Neither of them knew when to shut up. Stanky was nicknamed "The Brat," and the moniker was well deserved. In his playing days it had been said of him: "He can't hit, he can't run, and he can't throw. All he can do is beat you." As a player he would do anything to get on base—he led the NL in walks three times—and as a manager he would do anything to get on your nerves.

But he went too far when he told the Chicago writers that Yaz was "a moody ballplayer" and "an All-Star from the neck down" a few days before we got there on June 6.

A few years later folk rocker Jim Croce would record a song with these lyrics:

You don't tug on Superman's cape

You don't spit in the wind

You don't pull the mask off the old Lone Ranger

And you don't mess around with Jim

Croce could have substituted Yaz for Jim, except that Yaz doesn't rhyme as well with wind. Eddie Stanky learned you don't mess around with Yaz. I guess he thought he could goad Yaz into trying too hard and get him to lose his focus. We were such a young team, and Yaz was our most experienced player. If he could get Yaz off his game, the rest of us would be rendered helpless. And Stanky did get Yaz ticked off. He wouldn't show it publicly, but boy, was he mad! Unfortunately for Stanky, 1967 was not the year to get on Yaz. Stanky backed off quickly but too late.

Yaz's bat was pretty quiet in the first game of the series. He got a single in four at-bats, and we lost 5–3. The next game was rained out, setting up a twi-night doubleheader the following evening.

I wasn't there. My wife, Elsie, had just given birth to our twin boys, Jimmy and Billy, back in Boston, and I had flown home to be with her. But here's what happened.

Yaz stroked a double and a single and drove in a run in the first game of the twi-nighter, but the White Sox won 5–2, leveling our record at 24–24. In the nightcap Yaz ripped four hits, including his 12th homer, and we won 7–3 to give Gary Bell a victory in his Red Sox debut.

After Yaz singled in the fourth inning for his third hit of the game, Stanky came out of the dugout to relieve Wilbur Wood. When he got to the mound, Stanky looked over at Yaz, put his hand up to his neck, and made a downward motion. The meaning of the gesture was obvious.

"You took a first-place team last year and managed it into fourth place. What are you going to do this year?" Yaz called to him.

"Having a big day, eh? You got a couple of hits?" Stanky responded.

"Wrong again!" Yaz hollered. "I got three."

When Yaz batted again in the sixth, he belted a 440-foot homer to center field, the deepest part of the old Comiskey Park. As he trotted around the bases, he saw Stanky standing on the top step of the dugout and tipped his cap to him. Stanky never criticized Yaz again.

"Maybe because we've been trying to get Yastrzemski out for two years and haven't, I was a little irritated," Stanky reflected later. "I've always said he was a helluva ballplayer."

The following evening the Red Sox were back home at Fenway, playing the Washington Senators in front of a crowd of 25,386. Gil Hodges, Washington's manager, was aware of Stanky's comments regarding Yaz and how Yaz had responded.

"I don't want to say anything to keep the guy mad," Hodges told the media before the game. "I'll do anything to tone him down."

He couldn't. Yaz hit two more homers, giving him six in his last 32 at-bats and upping his total to 14 for the season. He also made two sensational catches in left field off Mike Epstein and Bob Saverine.

FOY GETS ADVICE FROM YAZ

Joe Foy was mad, though. Not at Gil Hodges or Eddie Stanky, but at Dick Williams. Although he had lost the weight Williams had ordered him to lose, Foy still wasn't hitting up to expectations. With his batting average at .188 and with just four homers and 10 RBIs, Foy was benched as soon as Jerry Adair arrived. Williams started Adair at third, saying he hoped that might build a fire under Foy. Adair moved over to shortstop while I was home in Boston with my newly expanded family, and that got Foy back into the lineup at third for the twi-nighter against the White Sox. Foy had a single, double, homer, and three RBIs in the doubleheader but found himself right back on the bench the next night against the Senators when I returned to the club. Foy sat there and stewed for five innings.

Lonborg picked that night to have his worst start of the season to date, and with the Senators leading 6–2 in the fifth, Williams sent up Foy to pinch hit for Lonnie. Foy homered, triggering a four-run rally that tied the game, and then stayed in to play third and hit another homer in the eighth. We won the game 8–7.

Williams kept him in the lineup after that, and Foy went on a tear, hitting safely in 18 of 20 games. Joe was an unsung hero for us. I never thought he got enough credit for what he did. He was very popular with his teammates, and when he was hot, he could hit anybody. He wasn't a great defensive third baseman, and George Scott saved a lot of errors for him. But Foy wasn't alone in that respect; Boomer saved a lot of errors for everyone in the infield.

But it took more than an attitude adjustment to break Foy out of his slump. He also made some adjustments at the plate following a suggestion from Yaz after the doubleheader in Chicago. Yaz studied Foy from the on-deck circle that night and then approached him in the dugout.

"Joe, are you looking for walks or base hits?" Yaz asked him. "The way you're standing all crouched over at the plate, it looks like you're trying to get a walk."

"What do you mean," Joe said defensively.

"I mean you can't possibly hit the ball right the way you're swinging now. You have to get your hands up. And you have to stand up straight and get out of that crouch."

Because Williams had installed Mike Andrews as the number-two hitter in the lineup in 1967 and dropped Foy lower in the batting order, Yaz, who always batted third, had not noticed the difference in Joe's approach at the plate until that night in Chicago when Foy happened to bat second again.

"Last season Joe always batted second and I batted third," Yaz explained to the writers. "So hundreds of times during that season I was in the on-deck circle while he was hitting. Naturally I had a terrific picture in my mind of what Joe should look like at the plate. But this year he has been batting down in the lineup most of the time, and I wasn't concentrating on him at the plate the way I would have if I had been on deck."

Joe gave Yaz credit for discovering the flaws.

"Yaz is the guy who helped me get squared away," he told the writers. "I did what he told me, and I've been hitting the ball good ever since."

One of the great things about the players on the Red Sox that year was that we all loved to talk hitting. Tony C., Yaz, Boomer, Reggie Smith, me . . . that's about all any of us talked about when we were at the park. What made Yaz really great was that he wasn't just focused on himself. He focused on what other guys were doing, too. He was like an extra coach. Yaz was everything to us that year.

FANS PICK ON SOX OF A DIFFERENT COLOR

We split that four-game series with the Senators and then divided a two-game set with the Yankees. We were two-thirds of the way through a nine-game homestand, and we were treading water at 3–3 with the first-place White Sox coming to town and leading us by five games in the standings. We split a doubleheader with them the first day, and the Red Sox fans were merciless in their tormenting of Eddie Stanky because of his comments about Yaz. He got booed every time he showed his head, and every time he stepped out of the dugout to change a pitcher or argue a call, the fans pelted him with paper cups and whatever else they could find. It was a crazy scene. I have to say it was a pleasant change to watch a visiting team feel the wrath of Red Sox fans who had been giving it to us for the last few years. By then the fans were completely on our side, cheering us even when we were losing a game. Stanky claimed to be in fear of his life and threatened to sue the Red Sox if he were physically harmed.

"Mr. Yawkey, that great sportsman, cares more about the deer and pheasant on that farm he has in North (sic) Carolina than he does about the human flesh here on the ball field," Stanky sneered. "I talked to my wife on the phone this afternoon. I told her that if anything happens to me, she is to sue Mr. Yawkey, the American League, and Mr. Marvin Miller, our wonderful player representative, for a million dollars apiece."

THE RED SOX THEME SONG

Ask any Red Sox fan who was around in 1967 to pick the most memorable game of that year, and you'll almost certainly get one of half a dozen answers. Most will pick the final game of the regular season, when we beat the Twins to clinch the pennant. Some will pick the August game in which we battled back from an 8–0 deficit to beat the Angels on a homer by Jerry Adair. Or the game where Jose Tartabull, who had a weak throwing arm, somehow threw out Chicago's Ken Berry at the plate to preserve a 4–3 victory. Others will choose the night of the fight in Yankee Stadium. A few, because it was such a tragic night, will pick the game earlier in that August series with California when Tony Conigliaro got beaned. But many of them, I'm sure, will pick the game of June 15, for it was on that night that Red Sox fans, both young and old, truly began to believe in us. And we began to truly believe in ourselves.

We had been making it a habit of coming from behind to win games all season. But this time it was against the first-place White Sox, and it was the climax to an unbelievably tense and dramatic three-hour-and-22-minute game that kept the 16,775 fans at Fenway Park riveted to their seats and tens of thousands of others around New England glued to their radios.

Rookie Gary Waslewski, who had been called up from Toronto less than two weeks before, was making his second major-league start for us against Chicago's Bruce Howard, and they locked up in a scoreless duel through seven innings. Stanky sent up 40-year-old Smoky Burgess, one of the best pinch hitters in the business, to hit for Howard with the go-ahead run on second base in the top of the eighth inning. Burgess had led the league in pinch hits in both 1965 and 1966 was in the process of setting a major-league record for career pinch hits with 145 (a record broken by Manny Mota in 1979). Waslewski got him out on a flyball to right, and the White Sox didn't score. Ageless knuckleballer Hoyt Wilhelm, a future Hall of Famer, took over for Howard and struck out four in two innings of relief, and after nine it was still a 0–0 game.

Waslewski had won 18 games for Toronto in 1966 and been named the International League's Pitcher of the Year. He had been expected to contend for a spot in the Red Sox rotation in 1967 but had a poor spring.

"He can throw harder than he's shown," Williams grumbled every time Waslewski got hammered in Florida. What none of us knew then was that Waslewski had pulled a muscle in his shoulder but didn't tell anyone because he knew Williams' policy was to immediately farm out all pitchers with sore arms.

Now Waslewski was healthy again and throwing the way we had expected. But in the 10th he pulled a muscle in his back, and after giving up singles to Ron Hansen and Al Weis to open the inning, he left the game. John Wyatt relieved him and struck out pinch hitter Pete Ward. Dick Kenworthy pinch hit for Wilhelm, and on an 0-and-1 pitch pinch runner Ed Stroud tried to steal third and was cut down by catcher Russ Gibson. Umpire Larry Napp ruled that Kenworthy, who had tried to check his swing, had gone around on the pitch for strike two, and Kenworthy yelped. Out came Stanky to argue, and he was thrown out of the game, much to the delight of the Red Sox fans. It was Stanky's second ejection in as many games. Kenworthy struck out to end the inning.

Burgess came out to warm up John Buzhardt, the new Chicago pitcher, between innings and gave Napp some lip, and he was ejected, too. Buzhardt set down the side in order, and the game went to the 11th.

The White Sox finally scored after Walter "No Neck" Williams led off with a double. With Don Buford at the plate, first baseman George Scott crept in, looking for a bunt, only to see Buford take a full swing and hit a smash up the first-base line. Boomer made a sensational diving play to flag the ball down, preventing another double and retiring Buford as Williams halted at third. Wyatt reached back and fanned Tommy Agee, the AL's Rookie of the Year in 1966, for the second out. But Ken Berry, who was riding a 20-game hitting streak, dumped a single into right to put Chicago ahead 1–0.

It looked like we were doomed to suffer a heartbreaking loss when Yaz popped up and Boomer hit a soft line drive to first baseman Tom McCraw in the bottom of the inning. Foy gave the fans a glimmer of hope when he grounded a single to left, bringing up Conigliaro.

Tony was in an 11-for-49 funk since returning from the Army and had been dropped to sixth in the batting order by Williams.

Buzhardt got Tony to chase a couple of sliders out of the strike zone, and now the White Sox were one strike away from ending it. Tony laid off two more sliders, then took a fastball inside that knocked him off the plate and ran the count full. That pitch presumably set up Tony for another slider low and away. Only this time Tony reached down and . . . bang! The ball just kept going up, up, and up until it landed in the screen for a two-run homer, and in an instant we had turned certain defeat into a fantastic 2–1 victory. Fenway went nuts.

Nowadays it's expected that players will pour out of the dugout and gather around the plate to welcome home someone who has just hit a walkoff homer. Such spontaneous celebrations were almost unheard of back in the sixties and before, unless you were maybe Bobby Thomson or Bill Mazeroski and had just hit a home run that won a pennant or a World Series. This was Game No. 58 out of 162. But this victory was too emotional, too unexpected. In those days you waited until the guy who won the game got near the dugout, and then you'd all go out to congratulate him. You'd celebrate a little bit, but never the whole team at home plate. But we couldn't help ourselves, and we all raced out to greet Tony when he crossed the plate. Even Dick Williams couldn't resist joining the impromptu party.

Every Red Sox fan in New England felt the same elation, a giddy feeling they had not experienced in at least 15 years. Howell Stevens, an old-time baseball writer who had covered the Red Sox in their glory years when they were winning six pennants and five World Series from 1903–18, was at the game and crowed: "It was like the Red Sox games of 1912, like the Golden Age!" We were only 30–28 and in third place, four games out of first. But after that night the games started to become surreal, like chapters in a serialized fairy tale. We started to believe we could beat anybody.

That was the night "The Impossible Dream" season officially began, and the Red Sox had a new theme song. Not a sarcastic ditty penned to the melody of "Take Me Out to the Ball Game" this time, but an inspirational Broadway show tune. In New York "Man of La Mancha," based on the Cervantes novel *Don Quixote* about an idealistic self-styled Spanish knight who refuses to concede defeat, was in the third year of a hit seven-year run, and the most popular song from the musical was "The Impossible Dream." The *Boston Globe* used it in a headline the next morning, and the public adopted it. We would be described as the "Cardiac Kids" and in other flattering terms throughout that amazing 1967 season, but "The Impossible Dream" became our theme.

FOY ON FIRE

You might expect that such a dramatic win would be the catalyst for a lengthy winning streak, but exactly the opposite occurred. Maybe we were emotionally spent, but we went to Washington and lost three of four to the last-place Senators. All the losses were by a single run, including a 1–0 setback the night after we had beaten the White Sox. We were a .500 club again, 31–31 and in fourth place, 6 ½ games behind Chicago, when we arrived in New York on Sunday night, June 18. While the rest of the team checked into the hotel in Manhattan, Joe Foy took the subway to the Bronx to stay with his parents. As he was walking the few blocks from the subway station to his childhood home, a neighborhood boy recognized him and ran up to him. He wasn't looking for an autograph.

"Hey, Joe, you better get home!" the boy cried. "Your house is on fire!"

Foy hustled to the building and saw thick smoke pouring from the upper-story windows. His parents were still inside.

"My mother and father were running around trying to salvage things, and I had to talk them out of staying inside the place," Foy related. "We just stood outside and watched it burn."

Two nights later Foy, his bat still ablaze since his hitting tip from Yaz, broke up a scoreless pitching duel between Gary Bell and our old nemesis, Mel Stottlemyre, by bashing a fifth-inning grand slam that propelled us to a 7–1 win over the Yankees.

TAKE ME OUT TO THE BRAWL GAME

If that 11-inning victory over the White Sox the previous week officially marked the end of the Red Sox' long era as losers, our 8–1 victory over the Yankees on June 21 marked the day the Red Sox Country Club officially closed its doors. For more than a decade the Red Sox had fostered a well-deserved reputation as a group of players more concerned with padding their own personal statistics than winning games. It was a reputation we had been striving to shed under Dick Williams, and this was the game that finally bonded the Red Sox together as a team.

The Yankees, after a promising start to the season, had fallen into ninth place and were by now resigned to the fact they were going nowhere. I don't know what they were thinking that night, but they weren't thinking about playing baseball. Maybe the Yankees were resentful, unable to accept the cold reality that after having lorded it over the Red Sox for 45 years, the Red Sox were finally a better team than they were.

With a TV audience watching the game back in New England, we jumped all over rookie Thad Tillotson for four runs in the first inning. When Foy, who had hit the game-breaking grand slam the night before, came up in the second inning with two on, Tillotson threw three fastballs high and tight to him and then hit him in the helmet, just above the left temple, with his next pitch. Foy, fortunately, wasn't hurt. He didn't glare at Tillotson, make a gesture, or say anything to him. He just dusted himself off and trotted down to first base.

When Tillotson came to bat in the bottom of the second, however, Jim Lonborg drilled him right between the shoulder blades.

Tillotson was furious. As he walked down to first base, still toting his bat, he pointed it at Lonborg in a threatening manner and began talking trash. Foy raced over from third and yelled at him: "If you want to fight, fight me!" Nestor Chylak, the third base umpire, followed Foy and tried to restrain him, but it was too late. Both benches and bullpens emptied, and the brawl was on.

Reggie Smith rushed in from center field, upended Tillotson, and slammed him to the ground. Punches were being thrown all over the infield. Yankees first baseman Joe Pepitone and I sought each other out. We had both grown up in Brooklyn and knew each other, and we started playfully throwing grass and dirt at each other, waiting for things to settle down as they usually do quickly in baseball fights. Then I heard one of the Yankees screaming: "You could have ruined the guy's career!" Ruined Tillotson's career? He got hit in the back! Tillotson's pitch could have killed Foy! That got me itching. Pepitone and I began swinging at each other, and the next thing I knew we were at the bottom of a pile.

"Twenty guys are on top of me, and one guy keeps pulling my hair. That ticked me off more than anything," Pepitone complained later. Pepitone was one of the first ballplayers to use a portable hair dryer and was vain about his hair.

Elston Howard, Dooley Womack, and Hal Reniff all went after Smith. "Howard grabbed my leg, Womack my neck, and Reniff was on my back," he remembered. Charlie Sands blindsided Tony Conigliaro. "It should have been a 15-yard penalty," Tony later quipped.

Even Dick Williams got involved in the fracas, although he admitted afterwards that he "had to look both ways to see if I was going to get it more from my own players than the Yankees."

Williams had told us in spring training that he was "here to win, not make friends. I'll try to make some players win just to show me up." And maybe he didn't have many friends on the ball club. But he had certainly earned our respect.

Twelve special cops working security at Yankee Stadium came onto the field to try to break up the fights. One of them was my older brother Dave, who was always stationed in the Red Sox dugout when we played there so he and I could chat. One of the Yankees, John Kennedy, said he heard Dave yelling: "You hurt my brother, I'll break your leg! I'll kill all you guys!" The Yankees players were really upset about that, and from then on Dave was stationed in the upper deck at Yankee Stadium, as far away from the field as he could possibly be. You needed binoculars to see him up way up there. Poor Dave! He got a bum rap. For one thing, he was a Yankees fan. It was unimaginable that he'd say he'd kill any of them, and he didn't. In all that chaos I could hear his voice, and all he ever said was: "Where's my brother? Where's my brother? Pepitone, where's my brother?"

Order was restored after about five minutes, and, amazingly, no one got thrown out of the game. But tempers continued to flare. When Lonborg batted in the third, Tillotson plunked him with a pitch, and the benches emptied again. There was a lot of shoving and posturing, and threats were exchanged. But no punches were thrown. Lonborg brushed back Charley Smith in the fourth, then beaned pinch hitter Dick Howser in the fifth. That, Lonnie said, was an accident. He freely acknowledged having intentionally hit Tillotson, arguing, "I can't let him hit one of our guys that way." But when he hit Howser he said, "We were ahead 8–0. The pitch just slipped." Howser agreed that the beaning wasn't intentional. But that was the incident that finally prompted an official warning from the umpires, and the game settled down after that. We won 8–1, and we had sent a clear message to the rest of the league that we could not be intimidated.

Had we lost that game, we would have been back at .500 again. Now we were 33–31, and we would not be at .500 or below the rest of the way. We were on our way to fulfilling Dick Williams' brash prediction that the Red Sox would win more than they would lose.

Oh, yeah. The out-of-business Country Club lost one of its last few members three days later when Dick O'Connell sold Dennis Bennett to the New York Mets.

ON THE SIDELINES

I wish my brother Dave had been around two days later to somehow protect me from really getting hurt.

We were playing the Cleveland Indians at Fenway Park in front of a big crowd of 30,233 and won 8–4. I came up in the seventh inning with the bases loaded, and George Culver unleashed an 0-and-2 fastball high and tight. I threw my left arm up to protect my head, and the ball struck me in the wrist, right where your wristwatch would be, a very bad spot. The pain was immediate and intense. Growing up in Brooklyn I had been hit by almost everything you could imagine, even bricks. One time somebody hit me in the head with a pipe. And still I had never experienced pain like this. I had never broken a bone in my life, but I was sure my wrist was broken. It felt like the bone had split straight up and down into two different bones.

They took me across the Charles River to Sancta Maria Hospital in Cambridge for X-rays, and fortunately the wrist was not broken. I had suffered only a deep bone bruise, but the doctors put a lightweight cast on my arm anyway. The purpose of the cast was to immobilize the joint and reduce the pain, but it didn't work very well. The pain in my wrist was so intense that when I got back to Fenway Park our trainer, Buddy LeRoux, had to wash the pine tar off my hand for me. I couldn't have done it myself without passing out.

I knew my wife, Elsie, had probably been listening to the game on the radio and would be worried. I wanted to call her and tell her I was okay. Buddy shoved the telephone over to me, and with my good hand I lifted the receiver out of the cradle. And then I suddenly realized we had just moved into a new house, and I didn't know the phone number!

The prognosis was that I would be out of the lineup for at least a week. What a bummer! I was off to the best start of my major-league career. I was hitting .296, ranking me eighth in the league in batting, with eight homers and 32 runs batted in. We were in the thick of a pennant race, and now I couldn't play for a while.

That week stretched into almost two. On June 27, my 24th birthday and four days after Culver hit me, I got the news I had been elected to the American League All-Star team as the starting shortstop. The managers, coaches, and players did the voting for the All-Star teams in those days. I had garnered 122 votes from my peers, more than twice as many as California Angels shortstop Jim Fregosi, who got 58. Yaz was also elected to the team. But as the All-Star Game drew closer and my wrist wasn't getting any better, I began to doubt I'd be healthy enough to play. I told everyone that if I wasn't back in the lineup before the All-Star break, I wasn't going to play in the game.

A SACRIFICE AT THE ALTAR OF BASEBALL

Jerry Adair filled in for me at shortstop while I was recovering from my injury and played great. But near the end of the month Dalton Jones had to leave for two weeks of training with the Army Reserves, and we were short another infielder. On June 29 the Red Sox reached all the way down to Class A ball and called up 19-year-old Ken Poulsen from Winston-Salem of the Carolina League.

Poulsen was scheduled to be married the next morning in Winston-Salem, North Carolina. His parents had already flown in from California, as had the parents of his bride-to-be, Vicki Swaton. The flowers and cake had been ordered, a photographer hired, a pastor scheduled, and 25 guests had been invited who were either already there or on their way. Everything had to be postponed as Poulsen dashed to the airport to catch a plane and join the Red Sox in Kansas City.

"We can always get married," a remarkably understanding Vicki said proudly. "But how often does a guy get sent up to the big leagues?"

In Poulsen's case, only once. Poulsen got into five games for the Red Sox, going 1-for-5 with a double before being sent back to the minors when I returned to the lineup. He never played in the majors again.

But Ken and Vicki did get married, so the story did end happily ever after.

WHEN BAD BREAKS BECOME GOOD BREAKS

On the final day of June Tony Conigliaro received word from Baltimore manager Hank Bauer, who would be managing the AL All-Star team, that he had been added to the squad. For Tony, like me, it was going to be his first All-Star Game, and naturally he was thrilled.

The spot had opened up for Tony because two of the league's All-Star outfielders—and future Hall of Famers—had been injured on the same day. Baltimore's Frank Robinson, who had won the Triple Crown and Most Valuable Player Award the previous summer, had suffered a severe concussion in a collision while running the bases. Detroit's Al Kaline, in a fit of pique, broke a finger slamming his bat into the rack.

Not only were these injuries a good break for Tony C., they were a huge break for the Red Sox. Both Robinson and Kaline were among the league's top hitters and run producers and would be lost to their respective teams for a month. The absence of Kaline, who was third in the league in hitting with a .328 average, third in RBIs with 53, and fifth in homers with 15, would keep the second-place Tigers within striking distance. (A year later they would win it all.) Robinson was bidding for his second straight Triple Crown, leading the AL in batting with a .337 mark and in RBIs with 59 and with 21 homers was one behind Harmon Killebrew. F. Robbie's unavailability would keep the defending world champion Orioles from climbing back into the pennant race. When you talk about an "Impossible Dream," it doesn't just happen because of the things you do personally on the field. Things that happen elsewhere also have an impact, and those two guys were the hearts of their teams. Naturally, we didn't know then exactly how long Kaline and Robinson were going to be sidelined. But, in retrospect, it was like divine intervention, that God wanted us, the 100–1 shots, to win this thing.

Conigliaro celebrated his selection to the All-Star team by hitting a monstrous three-run homer in the sixth inning that snapped a 1–1 deadlock and powered us to a 5–3 triumph over the Athletics in Kansas City. Gary Bell got the victory, his fifth of the month since being traded to the Red Sox. We finished June with a 37–34 record, putting us in third place, 5 ½ games behind the White Sox.

6

JULY 1967

It was an indication of how much we had improved as a team that it was rare for us to be blown out of a game anymore. Virtually every game we lost we had a chance to win until the final out. From mid-June through the first week of July our record was 12–10 . . . and all 10 losses were by the margin of a single run. At that juncture, 18 of our 37 losses had been by one run, and one-run losses can be frustrating. By then, however, it was simply frustrating to lose, whether it was by one run or a lot. After years of losing, we just hated to lose. When that streak of one-run losses ended on July 8, our defeat at the hands of Denny McLain and the Detroit Tigers was no more or less palatable. The score was 2–0.

Lonborg was named to the All-Star team on July 1, giving the Red Sox four All-Stars. He celebrated by becoming the first AL pitcher to win 10 games that season, raising his record to 10–3 by beating the Kansas City A's 10–2. Lonnie was also leading the league with 120 strikeouts in 125 innings.

Carl Yastrzemski had begun a remarkable streak at the end of April, reaching base safely with a hit or walk in 56 consecutive games until being stopped by the Athletics on July 2. It was only the third time all season Yaz had been kept off the bases.

Interestingly, all three times it had happened against the Athletics, who had the worst pitching staff in the league.

A SPARK IN THE BULLPEN

Rookie Billy Rohr, whose only two victories were over the New York Yankees back in April, had been sent back to the minors in late June. Called up from Toronto in early July was a character who would have fit in perfectly with the old fun-loving Country Club Red Sox, left-handed pitcher Sparky Lyle. The difference between Lyle and most of the old country clubbers was that Lyle could pitch, and in the 1970s he became one of the dominant closers in the game.

The Red Sox had drafted him out of the Baltimore organization in 1964. Lyle threw extremely hard and had a wicked slider, but he was not yet 23 years old when the Red Sox called him up, and he still hadn't mastered all his pitches. He stayed with us the rest of the year and pitched in 27 games, going 1–2 with five saves and a 2.30 ERA. But Dick Williams was careful about picking the right spots to use him. Later Lyle would twice lead the American League in saves, and in 1977, after he had been traded to the Yankees, he would win the Cy Young Award.

Lyle would later develop a reputation for plunging nude into birthday cakes that fans had sent to the clubhouse. But he was kind of quiet when he first joined us. As he contributed more, he began to open up and joke around more.

The Red Sox were in Anaheim when Lyle arrived. I was eating breakfast in the hotel restaurant when I saw him trying to check in. His room wasn't ready yet, so he stored his bags in a room behind the front desk. We chatted for a while, and then I went up to my room. I didn't see Sparky again until the next day, and he was wearing the same clothes I'd seen him wearing the day before. His bags were still stowed behind the desk. I think he got bored waiting for his room, left to check out the female talent in Southern California, and never came back to the hotel.

GUTS AND GLORY: THE RYAN FAMILY

Mike Ryan wasn't much of a hitter. But he could catch and throw, and Dick Williams liked to catch him against teams like the White Sox and Athletics, who ran every time they got the chance. So Ryan, who was hitting .247 with one homer and 12 RBIs, was behind the plate when we swept a three-game series from the A's in Kansas City June 30-July 2. The A's, who led the league with 132 steals in 1967, didn't swipe a single base in the series.

In the second game of the series, Ryan dislocated a finger when he tried to make a barehanded catch of an errant pitch from Lonborg. His mitt had slipped off while reaching for the ball. That night the pain was so bad he couldn't sleep. But he told Williams he wanted to catch the next day's game anyway. Trainer Buddy LeRoux rigged up some kind of splint for him, but there wasn't much he could do to alleviate the pain.

When the writers wanted to portray him as some sort of hero after the game, Ryan tried to discourage them. His 20-year-old brother, Steven, was a lance corporal with the Marines in Vietnam and was often in combat.

"Catching with a broken finger doesn't rate very high in our family right now," Ryan explained. "Steven has just been recommended for a decoration for bravery in Vietnam. He was radio reconnaissance in some heavy fighting 20 miles from Da Nang. They were pinned down on four sides for several hours. Steve's squad leader was shot down beside him. Steve called for the choppers and administered first aid to his squad leader. When the choppers came, they were under heavy fire. He directed them back and later directed them in again."

Mike Ryan knew how to keep things in perspective.

Catcher Mike Ryan never thought of himself as a hero—not when his brother Steven was fighting in the jungles in Vietnam. (*Courtesy of the Boston Red Sox*)

READY OR NOT

I returned to the lineup on July 5 after having missed 12 days. I wasn't really ready. I could throw the ball with no problems, but swinging a bat was still an ordeal.

"If we waited for 100-percent recovery," Buddy LeRoux said, "he couldn't play until August."

My wrist was sore for the rest of the year. There was a little click in there every time I swung. An elbow, a knee . . . those injuries would have healed eventually. But no, it had to be my wrist. I couldn't take batting practice for the longest time, and when you can't take BP, you lose your edge, and then you lose your timing and quickness. I tried to gain that back, but I never did. I was never able to get it going again at the plate. I went 2-for-11, both singles, with one RBI in four games before the All-Star break.

YAZ—AND POP—CALLS HIS SHOT

We had lost five in a row, our longest losing streak of the season, heading into the last game before the All-Star break, the second game of a doubleheader in Detroit. The 10–4 loss to the Tigers in the first game marked the first time we had lost by so many runs since a 10–0 rout at the hands of the Orioles in late May.

Jim Lonborg and John Wyatt, pitching on an incredibly hot and muggy afternoon, combined to shut out the Tigers 3–0 in the nightcap and give us a sorely needed victory. Lonborg blacked out from the heat on the mound in the sixth inning but somehow made it through seven before Williams, after listening to Lonnie "babbling about some play that took place a few innings before" when he returned to the dugout, mercifully took him out of the game.

"I was out of it," Lonnie said. "It was so hot I couldn't concentrate, and everything was hazy. Actually, I was incoherent."

Lonborg, like every team's ace in that era, was a horse. Aces were expected to take the ball and go the distance. Complete games were the goal of all pitchers. Lonborg, for example, threw 170 pitches in that 8–1 brawl game against the Yankees in June. Yeah, they counted pitches back then. But pitchers weren't limited by pitch counts. Luis Tiant threw 163 pitches for us while beating the Cincinnati Reds 5–4 in Game 4 of the 1975 World Series. It wasn't unusual for Nolan Ryan to throw upwards of 200 pitches a game, and he pitched in the majors for 27 seasons, until he was nearly 47 years old!

Al Lakeman, our bullpen coach, had a pregame ritual with our starting pitchers. He'd hand them the game ball and tell them: "Give it back to me at the end of nine."

Yaz capped the victory with an eighth-inning home run in his last at-bat before the break and, with the assistance of third base coach Eddie Popowski, called his shot the way Babe Ruth allegedly did in Chicago during the 1932 World Series.

"When we were sitting in the dugout," Dick Williams recalled, "Yaz said he thought he had enough left in him for a long one. I guessed he'd hit it deep to right. But Pop said it would probably be to left field because Yaz was tired and would probably be late with his swing."

Yaz, as Pop predicted, lashed the ball into the left-field seats at Tiger Stadium, his 19th homer of the season and his fifth hit of the doubleheader.

THE ALL-STAR GAME

The All-Star break couldn't have come at a better time for us. We had lost five of our last six before the break and had slipped to 41–39. We had fallen into fifth place, six games behind the White Sox. Dick Williams, however, was optimistic about the second half.

"Now we're going into the second half two over and the best schedule in the league at home the last half," he noted. "Our guys really need the rest now. But I expect us to bounce back and play better than we have been."

While the rest of the team flew east for the traditional annual Red Sox family clambake on Cape Cod, Yaz, Tony C., Lonnie, and I flew west to Anaheim for the All-Star Game. The Red Sox would have three of the nine starting players for the American League in the game. Yaz would be starting in left, Tony in right, and I would be at shortstop. That was a tribute to just how far the Red Sox had come as a team in such a short time. A year ago we were struggling to stay out of last place, and now we were in the thick of the pennant race with four All-Stars and one-third of the AL's starting lineup!

Being surrounded by so many great players in the clubhouse was overwhelming. But the sight that awed me most was Mickey Mantle. My older brother Vince used to take me to games at Yankee Stadium, a 40-minute subway ride from Brooklyn, when I was real young. The Yankees were always playing the Red Sox, by the way, and for a while there I was beginning to think the Yankees and the Red Sox were the only two teams in the American League. Anyway, my favorite players were Yogi Berra, Elston Howard, and Mantle. Mantle was number one with me. He was near the end of the line now, and 14 ½ months later I would catch the ball in the last at-bat of his Hall of Fame career. Mantle's body was so beat up the trainers had to wrap him in adhesive tape. It took almost a half-hour, and when they were finished he looked like a mummy! And he had to go through this every single day!

I batted in the third inning against San Francisco's Juan Marichal, another future Hall of Famer, and popped up. Hank Bauer, the manager, knew how sore my wrist was and took me out of the game. So I was in the clubhouse when Mantle limped back in two innings later. He had just pinch hit for pitcher

Jim McGlothlin and looked at a third strike from Ferguson Jenkins. Now the trainers had to peel all that tape off him. Mantle showered and dressed and then left for the airport to catch a plane back to New York. I couldn't help but admire the guy. Here was one of the greatest players in baseball history, in constant pain, who had flown 3,000 miles and spent a half-hour getting taped from head to toe just so he could bat one time and was now going through the entire scenario in reverse. And he never complained.

Mantle was gone, but I had to sit in that clubhouse for a long, long time. A superstar like Mantle could leave early. Younger players like me had to stick around in case the press wanted to interview us afterward. The game went 15 innings, the longest game in All-Star history, before Cincinnati's Tony Perez won it for the National League with a homer off Kansas City's Catfish Hunter, who pitched the last five innings. The final score was 2–1, and it was one of the dullest games ever. Philadelphia's Richie Allen and Baltimore's Brooks Robinson had also homered, but there had been only 17 total hits in the game while the pitchers racked up 30 strikeouts.

Yaz, who was always at his best in All-Star Games, had gotten on base five times, collecting three of the AL's eight hits and both its walks. Tony C., who would be playing in the only All-Star Game of his career, played all 15 innings and went 0-for-6 but made a pretty catch in right field of a drive off the bat of San Francisco's Orlando Cepeda in the 10th. Lonborg didn't pitch because he had worked on Sunday, two days earlier, and Bauer feared his stuff might be marginal.

THE STREAK

We split a doubleheader with the Orioles right after the All-Star break, getting walloped 10–0 in the second game. It would be the last game we would lose for ten days. We launched a 10-game winning streak—the longest by a Red Sox team in 16 years—the next day that would carry us almost to the top of the standings.

I spent most of that time cheering from the dugout. My wrist was killing me. As soon as I got back from Anaheim, I had cortisone injections three straight days. I played three games before my wrist swelled up, and then I came out of the lineup.

Some people—though not my teammates—all but accused me of being a malingerer. This bothered me tremendously. The year before I had come out of the lineup with an imbedded cyst in my lower back that Doc Tom Tierney, the club physician, couldn't see, and I was accused of jaking it then. Billy Herman, who didn't like me anyway, kept hinting to the press that I didn't want to play. The gossip didn't stop until the pain got so bad I ended up in the hospital, where the doctors there discovered the cyst. When Herman got fired shortly after that, I was both stunned and hurt to read a headline in the *Boston Herald*: "Herman says Petrocelli got him fired." What did I do to deserve to have that on my conscience?

Now I was hearing the same stuff all over again. It was all nonsense. Why wouldn't I have wanted to play? I had been among the league's top ten hitters most of the season, the team was hot, and we were in the thick of a pennant race. I kept being told I had to play through the pain. But nobody knew just how much pain I was in. I couldn't play.

The streak began on July 14 in front of a crowd of 27,787 at Fenway Park. Yaz matched his career high with his 20th homer, and Tony C. hit a tape-measure shot over everything in left as we routed the Orioles 11–5. I had a two-run double that put us ahead 8–0 in the fourth before Dick Williams mercifully took me out of the game.

I had my third cortisone shot in as many days the next morning and wasn't in the starting lineup that afternoon. Joe Foy started a triple play in the first inning, and we quickly built up a 5–1 lead. But Dalton Jones was away for two weeks with the Army, and we were short an infielder. So when Mike Andrews banged up his hip trying to make a tag play at second on Brooks Robinson and had to leave the game, Adair took over at second, and I had to go in and play shortstop. I could catch the ball and throw it. I just couldn't hit it with any authority. We won 5–1, and that was my last appearance for a week. It was frustrating. I had gotten off to a great start, and when you're not in the lineup you don't feel quite as close to the guys because you're not doing anything to help the team. Fortunately, the Red Sox didn't need me at all, and I was happy to see us doing well. I just wanted to be a bigger part of it. The main focus, as it should be, was on winning, and with each win we gained more and more confidence. By the end of the streak we truly believed we had a shot to win this thing. We felt we could beat any of the other clubs.

The Detroit Tigers, who had lost five in a row, came into Fenway for a pair of games. We stretched their losing streak to seven and extended our winning streak to four.

Yaz socked his 21st homer to establish a career high, and Tony belted his 15th as we won the first game 9–5 and pulled into a third-place tie with the Tigers. Yaz hit another homer the next day, added a double, and knocked in three runs in a 7–1 victory over the Tigers. It was only mid-July, barely halfway through the season, and Yaz was hitting .328 with 22 homers and 65 RBIs. He was second to the injured Frank Robinson in batting, third in homers, and second in RBIs, one behind Harmon Killebrew. Not only was he in a position to challenge for the Triple Crown, the Boston press was beginning to tout him as the league's Most Valuable Player. Yaz didn't want to hear that kind of talk.

"It's bull when people say one person can carry a club," he argued. "If Andrews and Foy don't get on, I can't drive in any runs. If Conigliaro doesn't hit, I can't score any. People look at individual performances. But all 25 guys have to contribute. Sure, you always want to be the best. Maybe I'm not as strong as Frank

Robinson. I know I'll never hit 40 or 50 home runs. But maybe I can catch the ball and run a little bit better to offset that."

He didn't know it then, but Yaz was selling himself short. Way short.

We hit the road for six games, where your objective is to break even. One of the time-worn formulae for winning a pennant is to win half your games on the road and two-thirds of your games at home. That works out to a .600 winning percentage, which is usually good enough to finish first.

We won them all.

The trip started in Baltimore where Lonborg pitched a five-hitter with 11 strikeouts and helped his own cause with an RBI single during a five-run second inning. The final score was 6–2. Mike Andrews belted a three-run homer to ignite a five-run fifth the next night as we beat the Orioles again, 6–4. We were ahead 2–0 in the third inning of the third game of the series when it got rained out.

The next stop was Cleveland. Joe Foy clubbed a three-run homer in the third off Luis Tiant that propelled us to a 6–2 victory over the Indians, and we hurdled the Minnesota Twins into second place, just 1 ½ games behind the White Sox. We pulled within a half-game the next day as Lee Stange needed just 83 pitches to shut out the Indians 4–0 and Andrews provided him with the only run he'd need with a leadoff homer.

A Sunday doubleheader on July 23 wrapped up the trip. Lonborg was scheduled to pitch the first game, but for a while it looked like he might miss the assignment. The day before he had been standing in the outfield with his back to the cage while the Indians were taking batting practice, and Vic Davalillo had hit him in the shoulder with a line drive. The shoulder had stiffened overnight. But it loosened up enough for him to take the mound, and he pitched a seven-hitter with 11 strikeouts to run his record to 14–3. Tony Conigliaro swatted a two-run homer in the first inning, making him at the age of 22 years, six months, and 16 days the youngest player in American League history and second youngest in major-league history after Mel Ott to reach 100 career homers. For the second time in three days Foy hit a homer—this one a grand slam in the second inning—off Tiant, who had a rubber arm in those days and was starting on one day's rest after lasting just three innings in his previous outing, and we coasted to an 8–5 win. I tested my wrist during the last three innings, replacing Adair at shortstop and doubling in my only at-bat, but it was still sore as heck. Gary Bell beat his former Cleveland teammates 5–1 in the nightcap, throwing a five-hitter. Reggie Smith scored the winning run by pilfering home on the front end of a double steal in the fourth, and Tony C. hit another homer in the fifth.

Ten in a row. In recent years the Red Sox had had trouble winning that many in a month. How well were we playing? Six of the last seven wins had been complete games, and we hadn't made an error in the last 67 innings. We outscored our opponents 67–26 during the streak. Everybody was hitting and delivering in the clutch, and we were 52–40 and within a half-game of first place.

"Other teams aren't taking us for granted no more," Foy said. "Used to be they'd go out there with an it's-just-another-ballgame attitude against us. Now they're worrying about us as much as anyone else in this league."

Were we having fun? You bet.

"When you're winning, it's more like a game," Yaz mused. "When you're losing, it's a business."

As strict a disciplinarian as Dick Williams was, he let us have fun in the clubhouse, and we did have a lot of laughs. As we kept on winning and dared to let ourselves dream about winning the pennant, Foy, for example, talked about buying a "hog" with his share of the World Series money. A "hog" in Foy's parlance was a Cadillac. When someone made a game-ending out with the winning run on base, Foy would say something like: "Hey! You just took the steering wheel out of my hands!" What made the gag even funnier was that Foy, who had grown up in the Bronx, didn't even have a driver's license, much less own a car. Boomer had let him drive his car once while we were in spring training and said Foy was absolutely terrible behind the wheel.

Williams didn't mind us joking around in the dugout . . . as long as we were winning. But when we were losing—and even sometimes when we were winning—he'd pace the dugout and suddenly stop and ask somebody how many outs there were. Sometimes someone who hadn't been paying attention would stutter: "Uh . . . uh . . ." and try to peek at the scoreboard. Too late!

Manager Dick Williams was much friendlier with Red Sox fans than he was with his players. He didn't care if the players liked him or not; he only cared if we won or lost. (*Courtesy of the Boston Red Sox*)

Dick wouldn't get angry. He'd just say: "Pay attention to the game, and don't let it happen again." He wanted us focused on the game, even when we weren't playing.

Not everyone was sharing our euphoria about the 10-game winning streak, however. Gabe Paul, the Indians' general manager, cautioned: "Enjoy yourselves while you can. Remember, the cream of today is the cheese of tomorrow."

White Sox manager Eddie Stanky, whose team was only a half-game ahead of us in the standings, sniffed: "I don't see all this excitement over Boston. It's normal for a team to go on a hot streak. We won 10 in a row back in May, and nobody made a big deal out of us."

THE HOMECOMING

The winning streak was a big deal back in Boston, though. As we boarded our United Air Lines charter at Cleveland's Hopkins Airport, we had no clue about the reception that was awaiting us at Boston's Logan Airport. While we were on the road sweeping Baltimore and Cleveland, pennant fever was sweeping New England for the first time since the late 1940s. We were making our descent into Boston when the captain got on the horn and informed us: "Fellows, we're not going to be able to let you go through the gate to the baggage claim. You've got a crowd there of 10-, 15,000 people to welcome you." We collectively said: "What? Holy Jeez! This is great!"

As many as 15,000 fans were clogging the corridors and disrupting foot traffic so badly that travelers were missing their flights. Hundreds had even camped out on one of the runways. Not even the arrival of The Beatles for their 1966 concert at Suffolk Downs had paralyzed Logan like this. John Lennon had once said that The Beatles were more popular than God. Right now, the Red Sox were more popular than The Beatles! Airport officials instructed the pilot to taxi the aircraft to the Butler Aviation hangar at a remote part of the airport. There we would be met by the bus to take us to Fenway, where our cars were parked.

Some of the fans must have gotten wind of the change in plans, because a couple hundred of them were there to cheer us when we got off the plane and boarded the bus. Then the mob began rocking the bus, making us feel like we were trapped dictators in some South American banana republic. It was scary yet exhilarating at the same time. We talked among ourselves and said: “What the heck are we doing? Fifteen thousand people took the trouble to come down here to welcome us home. Shouldn’t we at least acknowledge their devotion and say hello?” We spontaneously decided the bus should take us to the gate so we could go through the terminal just like we always did. I’m sure airport security and the state police weren’t happy about that, but they let us do it. What a mob scene! We thought they might at least rope off a path for us, but there was nothing to separate us from the crowds. We could barely move. Everyone wanted to pat us on the back and shake our hands. The whole scene was absolutely incredible. It was nine, ten o’clock at night, and fathers were there with their infants on their shoulders! What a difference from a decade earlier when the Red Sox had landed at Logan, returning from yet another bad road trip, and before stepping off the plane pitcher Frank Sullivan had quipped: “Scatter when you leave, men, so they don’t get us all with one burst.”

After that insane night, the Red Sox no longer publicly announced their travel itinerary.

YOU CAN’T WIN ’EM ALL

By now we were being compared to the “Whiz Kids,” the young 1950 Philadelphia Phillies team that had won the National League pennant. It really wasn’t a good comparison. For one thing, those

Phillies were old geezers compared to us. The average age of the "Whiz Kids" was 26 ½, a good two to three years older than the average age of the 1967 Red Sox. For another, the Phillies had finished third in 1949 with an 81–73 record. Even though the Phillies hadn't won the pennant since 1915, it couldn't have been that much of a shock that they contended again with almost the same lineup in 1950 and won. We had finished ninth in 1966, and the Red Sox hadn't finished as high as third since 1958.

Dick Williams refused to get caught up in the hullabaloo. Asked repeatedly if he thought the Red Sox were going to win the pennant, he stuck to his preseason prediction. "We'll win more than we lose," he reiterated. "That's as far as I want to go at the minute."

To some extent, we became the victims of our own success. We were back home to play the third-place California Angels, who were almost as hot as we were. They had won six in a row and were 33–12 since early June, beginning their run shortly after we had swept that doubleheader from them. After the reception we got at Logan Airport, we expected to see 50,000 people trying to cram their way into tiny Fenway Park for the first game of the series. But a miscommunication from the PR department led fans to believe the game was sold out, and only 21,527 showed up to see the Angels end our winning streak and extend theirs. The Angels struck for three runs in the first inning against Gary Waslewski, and we could never quite catch up. We lost 6–4. I felt I was healthy enough to play now, but Williams was reluctant to break up a winning combo and let Jerry Adair stay at short. I did pinch hit in the seventh and was back in the starting lineup the following night.

A packed house of 32,403 was on hand this time, and we fell behind 4–1. George Brunet, a wily old veteran lefthander who was with his fifth major-league team, took a one-hitter into the seventh. But we thrilled the crowd by erupting for six runs that inning and won 9–6, ending California's streak at seven games.

An SRO throng of 34,193—the largest crowd at Fenway since Opening Day in 1958—turned out the next afternoon, and we rewarded them with a stirring comeback in the bottom of the ninth. Jim McGlothlin was in total command after giving up solo homers to Yaz and George Scott in the first two innings and had a 5–2 lead when we came to bat for possibly the last time in the game.

Sal Maglie, our pitching coach, surveyed the enthusiastic crowd and announced to the dugout: "Nobody's leaving the park. Let's win it for them."

Andrews led off the ninth with a single and Foy slammed a two-run homer into the screen to chase McGlothlin. One out later Conigliaro deposited another ball into the screen off reliever Bill Kelso and knotted the score at 5–5.

As impossible as it sounds, the drama heightened in the 10th. Yaz robbed pinch hitter Moose Skowron of a hit by making a catch of a sinking line drive while on a dead run. With two outs Bob Rodgers drilled a single to left, and Don Mincher tried to score from second only to be thrown out at the plate by Yaz. We won the game in the bottom of the inning when Reggie Smith led off with a triple and scored on an error by third baseman Paul Schaal.

California manager Bill Rigney was nearly inconsolable as he sat behind his desk in the visitor's clubhouse afterward. "The Red Sox broke my streak last night," he said softly. "But they broke my heart today."

We then lost three of five to the Twins and ended the month of July in second place, two games behind the White Sox. With two months to go, it was a five-team race with Detroit, Minnesota, and California also bunched within five games of the top.

7

AUGUST 1967

Now that we were in a pennant race, Red Sox general manager Dick O'Connell feverishly worked the phones to ensure we'd stay in it by acquiring useful spare parts for the roster. On July 16 he had purchased veteran Norm Siebern from the San Francisco Giants to pinch hit and back up George Scott at first base. Siebern had enjoyed a few productive years in the early 1960s for Kansas City, notably in 1962 when he hit .308 with 25 homers and 117 RBIs, but he was 34 and coming to the end of his career. He was hitting only .155 for the Giants as a part-timer but had played in two World Series for the Yankees in the late '50s and knew how to handle the pressures of a pennant race. Siebern, however, took his sweet time about reporting, saying he needed time to relocate his family, and didn't show up for a week. After arriving, though, he delivered a big two-out pinch single for us during a four-run rally in the eighth inning that wiped out a 3–2 Minnesota lead and gave us a 6–3 win over the Twins on July 29. Like so many others, winning that game was crucial in a pennant race that would be decided by a single game.

On August 3 O'Connell picked up another veteran with plenty of championship experience. The ninth-place Yankees put

38-year old catcher Elston Howard—another one of my boyhood heroes along with Mickey Mantle and Yogi Berra—on waivers, and O'Connell put in a claim. Every other team in the league except for the White Sox, who were ahead of us in the standings, had to pass on him before we could get him, and they did. But now O'Connell had to talk Howard out of retiring. Mr. Yawkey was in Chicago attending league meetings, and O'Connell asked him to place a personal call to Howard.

"I admit it. I wanted to finish my career with the Yankees," Howard said later. "When you talk to someone like that, it makes a difference. I never enjoyed a telephone call more in my life. Mr. Yawkey said to me: 'Elston, we want you in Boston, and we know that you can help our club, maybe to win the pennant.' He made everything all right."

Howard was hitting only .196 for the Yankees. In 1961 he had hit .348—which would have ranked him second in the league if he'd had enough at-bats to qualify—and swatted 21 homers. Two years later, when he hit .287 with 28 homers and 85 RBIs, he was the MVP of the American League. A nine-time All-Star who had played in nine World Series for the Yankees, Ellie wasn't swinging the bat the way he used to, and he wouldn't get the head of the bat out and hit the ball on the nose very often after we got him. But the man could still play defense. He knew the hitters in the league, he could catch and throw, and he was great at blocking balls. The ease with which he did things behind the plate just made everyone feel comfortable. Both Mike Ryan and Russ Gibson had been doing a terrific job for us. But when you can get a player of Elston Howard's ability to help you, you have to go get him.

"Howard is the best catcher I've ever seen for calling a ballgame," Carl Yastrzemski said when he learned of the deal. "He's the best handler of pitchers, the best at setting up a batter. Howard will help a young catcher like Mike Ryan simply by talking to him and giving him his ideas."

We didn't need four catchers, so O'Connell put Bob Tillman on waivers a few days later, and he was picked up by the Yankees.

Howard took a lot of good-natured grief from us for breaking up Billy Rohr's no-hitter back in April, and he would do most of our catching down the stretch. He would hit only .147, but he would give us exactly what Williams was looking for behind the plate. And he would be a key figure in one of our most unforgettable games.

THE RELUCTANT ACE

Jim Lonborg was our quid for Baltimore's quo, Jerry Adair. Whereas the Orioles had snatched Adair away from the clutches of the Red Sox in 1958, five years later the Red Sox exacted their revenge by stealing Lonborg from right beneath the noses of the Orioles. Now, fortunately, we had both of them, and they would be instrumental in helping us win the pennant.

Unlike most boys who play baseball, Lonborg didn't dream of playing in the major leagues someday. The son of a professor at Cal Tech, Lonnie was always more interested in academics than baseball. He didn't even make his high school team at San Luis Obispo until his junior year, and it didn't bother him. He emerged as the team's ace as a senior and then enrolled at Stanford in the pre-med program. He continued to play baseball in college and began attracting a lot of interest from major-league scouts. Most of them backed off, deeming him unsignable, when he told them he was adamant about becoming a surgeon. But the Orioles were confident that if they were patient enough they could convince him to sign a pro contract.

After Lonborg posted a 1.30 ERA and piled up the strikeouts during his junior year at Stanford, the Orioles arranged for him to play summer ball in Winner, South Dakota, for an amateur team in which they had a vested interest. Winner was about as remote an outpost as you could find in college summer ball, but the Orioles sent scout Phil Galvin to babysit Lonnie anyway.

"The Orioles were good to me," Lonborg said. "But I don't think they had a lot of money available to sign me. Jim Palmer was also on that team with me, and I'd heard he was getting a $100,000 bonus from them."

The Red Sox hadn't shown any interest in Lonborg until Bobby Doerr happened to see him pitch a game in Sturgis one night when he struck out 13 batters. A few days later Red Sox scout Danny Doyle—the same scout who had been burned by the Orioles with Jerry Adair—quietly drove into Winner and, armed with Mr. Yawkey's checkbook, knocked on the door of Lonborg's motel room, which was just a few doors away from Galvin's.

"He spoke to me bluntly," Lonnie remembered. "He asked me what I wanted. I said I wanted to finish my education and become a surgeon."

That wasn't the answer Doyle was looking for. He wasn't interested in knowing what Lonnie wanted; he already knew that. He was interested in knowing *what* Lonnie wanted. Lonnie told him he wanted $18,000 plus the rest of his education paid for, and Doyle wrote out a check.

"He offered me enough money, right there on the spot, to make me change my mind," Lonnie said.

Early the next morning Lonborg phoned Galvin with the bad news. "Phil, this is Jim Lonborg. I deeply appreciate what you have done for me. But the Red Sox last night, on a take-it-or-leave-it basis, offered me so much money I simply couldn't refuse it."

He finished up the class work for his degree in biology during the off-season, and now, four years later, he was pitching the Red Sox to an improbable pennant.

Private First Class Lonborg had to leave the Red Sox for two weeks of active duty with the Army at the end of July. It looked as if we were going to be without our ace until the middle of August,

The Red Sox stole Jim Lonborg right from under the noses of the Baltimore Orioles, thanks to Mr. Yawkey's checkbook. (*Courtesy of the Boston Red Sox*)

and we were all pretty glum about that. But although Lonnie was posted in Atlanta, he managed to get a pass every time he was scheduled to pitch for us and never missed an assignment, flying to Boston or wherever we were on the day of the game and flying back to Atlanta the next. He was also able to work out with the Braves at Fulton County Stadium during those two weeks to stay in playing shape.

Lonnie got his first pass on August 1. After getting up at five a.m. and performing his military clerical duties until early afternoon, he rushed to Hartsfield Airport in a car borrowed from Braves pitcher Jay Ritchie, who had come up with us in the Red Sox system before being traded with Lee Thomas and Arnold Earley for Dan Osinski and Bob Sadowski after the 1965 season. The flight to Boston was supposed to depart at 3:10 but was delayed, so Lonnie dropped into an airport restaurant and ordered a steak. Before it arrived, he heard the boarding call and dashed to the gate. The plane left Atlanta an hour late and landed at Logan Airport at 7:15, only 45 minutes before the second game of a day-night doubleheader against the Kansas City Athletics was scheduled to begin. Mr. Yawkey's chauffeur, George Cheney, was waiting for him and sped him to Fenway Park. At 7:46, PFC Lonborg was in a Red Sox uniform and warming up. Boy, were we glad to see him!

The last-place A's had already beaten us 4–3 in the day game. Dick Williams had earlier shipped out Gary Waslewski and called up Dave Morehead, who was 11–5 for Toronto with a 3.21 ERA and 109 strikeouts in 122 innings, and started him in that game. The Maple Leafs had been in Columbus, Ohio, when Morehead got the call and was ordered to fly directly to Boston. But he first went home to Toronto to collect his belongings and was late in reporting, ticking off the manager. Williams was even less happy with Morehead when he failed to record an out in the third inning, walking the first two batters and then surrendering three consecutive hits to account for all four K.C. runs. Asked by the press between games what he thought of Morehead's comeback performance, the manager snorted: "Not much." Then, alluding to

Morehead's side trip to Canada, Williams added: "Maybe he's not used to our operation. Maybe he thinks it's the way it used to be."

Lonborg, harried and hungry, wasn't sharp that night, either. "He looked like he was in a world of his own out there. His timing was way off," commented catcher Mike Ryan. Lonnie gave up eight hits and walked five batters in 5 ⅓ innings and was relieved after hitting Danny Cater in the head with a pitch. By then we had rallied from a 3–0 deficit to take a 4–3 lead, and while Sparky Lyle was finishing up with 3 ⅔ innings of hitless relief, Ryan put the game out of reach with a three-run homer in the seventh. We won 8–3, presenting Lonborg with his 15th victory.

WILLIAMS REVISES HIS PREDICTION

We ended up splitting that four-game series with the lowly Athletics and flew to Minnesota, where the new and improved Red Sox still couldn't figure out how to win. We were swept and scored just one run in the three games, wasting excellent pitching performances by Darrell Brandon, Lee Stange, and Lonborg. Our pitchers surrendered only seven runs in the series. Lonnie, pitching on another one-day pass, went up against Dean Chance, who authored a "perfect" game against us, retiring all 15 batters he faced before the remainder of the contest was washed out by rain. Fortunately, we didn't lose much ground to the White Sox, who led us by 2 ½ games. But the Twins pulled into a tie with us for second place.

We had a day off in Kansas City on August 7. I don't know why Dick Williams picked that day to reassess his preseason prediction about our chances, given the fact that we had just lost three of five to the Twins in Boston, split a four-game series at home to the last-place Athletics, and then been swept by the Twins in Minnesota. Maybe he said it just to buck up our spirits, his way of telling us that in spite of his insults and withering criticism he believed in us more than ever before. After having stuck firmly for four months to his vow back in March that the Red Sox would win more than they'd lose, Williams now predicted we'd win 90 games . . . and the pennant would be decided in the final two games of the season against the Twins at Fenway Park. Wow! Williams did a great imitation of a psychic that day. We had exactly 90 wins going into those last two games against the Twins, and the pennant was decided in that series.

FAR FROM THE MADDING CROWD

But we weren't playing like contenders in the first half of August. We managed to win two of three from the Athletics but were swept by the Angels in Anaheim—all one-run losses—and finished the road trip with a 2–7 record. That knocked us all the way back into fifth place, although we were only 2 ½ games behind the Twins, who had overhauled the White Sox.

George Scott and Joe Foy had been packing on some pounds again, and Dick Williams benched them both in Anaheim for being overweight. Boomer, who was four pounds over his limit, was slumping and only 2-for-15 on the road trip. But he had been our best hitter against the Angels all season with a .343 average, four homers, and nine RBIs, and he had hit homers in three straight games off California's Jim McGlothlin, who was starting the first game of the series. When the press pointed that out, Williams responded: "At what weight did Scott hit the homers off him?"

McGlothlin shut us out 1–0, the only run scoring on a wild pitch by Lee Stange. McGlothlin was certainly relieved to see Boomer sitting in the dugout.

"I was surprised to find Scott wasn't in the batting order . . . and happy, too," he said. Boomer did pinch hit for Stange in the eighth and drew the only walk McGlothlin issued all night. "I didn't really want to give Scott anything good," he admitted.

We were shocked by Dick's decision to bench Boomer and Joe. Here we were, battling for the pennant, and we thought for sure he'd cut those guys some slack. It wasn't like they were grossly overweight; it was just a couple of pounds. When we heard about it, we said: "Holy Jeez, how can he bench either one of those guys? They're such an integral part of the team." But, in retrospect, I have to give Williams credit for being consistent. In the past managers had said they were going to do this and do that, and then some time during the season they stopped doing it. Mid-season changes in philosophy leave a team confused. Remaining strictly faithful to his spring training philosophy was a matter of principle to Dick Williams.

"This is the way I've operated all season, and I'm not going to change now just because we're in the race," Williams declared. "How are you going to get all over a guy for breaking a rule if you'll let another guy get away with it?"

Boomer, to his credit, accepted his punishment with barely a whimper.

"I want to play even if I weigh 500 pounds," he said. "I'm a country boy, and I like to eat. But Dick Williams set a top playing weight for me of 215 pounds. I think that's a good playing weight. I know he does it for my good. And he's the boss, man."

Foy managed to sweat off five pounds in 24 hours and was back in the lineup the next day, driving in our only run in a 2–1 loss. Boomer, who could gain five pounds just by smelling food, stayed on the bench while the writers took their turns second-guessing the manager.

The writers, just as desperate as any long-suffering fan to see the Red Sox win a pennant, were far less understanding than we were and roasted Williams in the papers after we lost the last game of the series 3–2. I hit a two-run homer in the ninth to get us close, and Boomer came off the bench to deliver a pinch single, but we couldn't pull out a victory.

In the *Boston Globe*, Clif Keane wrote: "What would (Williams) have told Babe Ruth when the slugger used to grab a half-dozen hot dogs before he played and had a shape like a barrel? Would Dick have said: 'I don't care about Ruth or anyone else. We have weight charts, and when Babe drops 20 pounds, he'll play.'"

The *Globe's* Harold Kaese complained: "Nine teams have managers. The Red Sox have a dietician (sic). Nobody ever heard of a manager benching a regular for being too heavy in August of a hot pennant race, although in 1965 (Baltimore's) Hank Bauer fined Boog Powell $10 for every pound he was above 241. If the Sox do not win, we can all be sporting about it and say: 'It was worth losing the pennant just to get Boomer in shape.'"

What the writers did not grasp was that a manager could lose a pennant and maybe come back and win it the next year. But once a manager loses his club, he has no chance of winning. Ever. Reward alone is not enough of an incentive for everyone, not on a 25-man team with a multitude of personalities. A manager has to convince his players to play hard for him by whatever tactics work best, whether it's love, hate, or revenge. Indifference is fatal.

Although they were perceived as Williams' whipping boys, I don't believe Dick had anything personal against either Boomer or Joe. But by making examples of them, he sent the message to the rest of us that if we started getting lazy about executing fundamentals or doing the things he expected from us, we'd be benched, too. I think Dick singled them out because he knew that, on a very young and potentially fragile baseball team, Boomer and Joe were both strong enough as individuals to take it without being crushed.

We took the red-eye home from the West Coast, arriving at Logan Airport around 8:20 on the morning of August 14. Unlike our homecoming after our last trip, when we had won 10 in a row and been greeted by a mob of 15,000 fans, only a handful of people were waiting for us this time. Exactly three of them were fans. Everyone else was a family member.

THE RETURN OF THE THIN MAN

George Scott was back in the lineup for the start of the 12-game homestand. He had slaved all weekend to get his weight down to 215 and couldn't quite make it. Eddie Popowski, whose job it was to monitor the weight charts, knew we needed Boomer's bat and glove and that Dick Williams was not going to bend the rules. So Pop fudged Boomer's weight and told Dick he was under the limit. Did Dick know Pop was fudging? There's no doubt in my mind he knew, because Williams knew everything. I think the way it happened was Dick's plan all along. Pop respected Williams, and I can't imagine he'd tell a white lie to Dick just to get Boomer back in the lineup. By doing it this way, Dick kept his credibility intact.

Boomer, batting cleanup, socked a homer into the left-field screen in his first at-bat and later made a couple of slick plays in the field. Dave Morehead shut out the Detroit Tigers 4–0 for his first complete game in the majors since his no-hitter almost two years earlier. Boomer slugged two more homers off Denny McLain the next day, driving in four runs and powering us to an 8–3 triumph. He continued his lusty hitting in the last game of the series, getting two hits and scoring a pair of runs. But we lost in 10 innings, 7–4, disappointing a crowd of 28,653 that put us over the million mark in attendance for the first time in seven years.

TRAGEDY

Tony Conigliaro had it all: tremendous talent, matinee idol looks, charisma, and personality. The only thing he didn't have was luck, and in the end that killed him.

An eligible bachelor, Tony C. was easily the most popular player on the Red Sox, especially with the ladies. He certainly took pleasure in their company. But while he dated actresses and Playboy bunnies, he wasn't a playboy like Bo Belinsky, who had achieved instant stardom by throwing a no-hitter for the Angels in his rookie year in 1962, begun dating buxom actress Mamie Van Doren, and before he was 30 had left the best years of his career in bars and boudoirs and was struggling to hang on in the majors. Tony didn't like to go to fancy nightclubs. In fact, he preferred to stay out of the public eye as much as possible.

When the Red Sox were on the road, Tony, Mike Ryan, and I liked to stay in our hotel rooms and practice singing three-part harmonies, the kind of doo-wop songs you might have heard sung on city street corners in the 1950s. Mike was usually off key. Tony would grimace, shake his head, and say: "Roomie, you gotta work on that or we're going to fire you from the group!" And Mike would assure him: "No, no! I'll work on it! I'll work on it!"

Tony had been signed to a recording contract and cut a few records. He'd be a guest on TV shows when he had the chance, and when he'd come back we'd ask him what it was like to be on TV with Merv Griffin, and he'd excitedly tell us all about it. I'm sure a lot of fans thought that Tony was full of himself and probably imagined that when he was at the ballpark he'd grab a bat and use it like a microphone. Nothing could have been further from the truth. Once Tony got to the park he'd leave all that extracurricular stuff behind him and focus on the game. He loved to hit, and the first thing he'd do was get his bat, start feeling it, and maybe bone it a little. Once he put on that Red Sox uniform, he was ready to play baseball. He had great concentration that way. Nothing distracted him.

At the age of 19 he'd jumped all the way from the lowest minor league to the majors, and at the age of 20 he'd led the American League in homers. By the time he was 22 he'd become the youngest player in AL history and second-youngest player in major-league history to hit 100 career homers. That Tony would eventually slug 500 homers and hit his way into the Hall of Fame was a foregone conclusion, and if he had just been able to stay away from all those broken bones it would have come to pass. But Tony was not only a chick magnet, he was a magnet for stray pitches. Five times he had bones broken by pitches, including the one that broke his shoulder blade five months earlier in spring training. He always recovered quickly, and he never showed any fear at the plate. But the pitch that hit him on the night of August 18 fractured his cheekbone, nearly blinded him, and crushed his career. He wasn't even 23 years old yet, and, except for a miraculous comeback that degenerated into a cruel two-year tease, his baseball career was effectively over and his life would never be the same.

It was a steamy Friday night with a near-capacity crowd of 31,027 on hand to see the first game of a four-game set with the Angels, who had just swept us in Anaheim the previous weekend. Gary Bell had retired the first 12 Angels in order when we came to bat in the bottom of the fourth against Jack Hamilton, a hard-throwing right-hander with a spitball and an acceptable reputation for coming in on hitters. Hamilton had allowed only one hit in the first three innings, a single by Conigliaro.

George Scott led off the fourth with a single but was thrown out trying to stretch it into a double. Some wise guy threw a smoke bomb from the stands into left field, and the game was delayed for about 10 minutes while we waited for the air to clear. Did that delay get Hamilton out of his rhythm? We'll never know. Finally Reggie Smith stepped into the box and flied to center for the second out. Tony set himself in the batter's box, crowding the plate as always, while I knelt in the on-deck circle. I always believed there was a spot where Tony couldn't see the inside pitch. If you threw it to the right spot, he'd hit that ball nine miles. But then there was this blind spot, a little more inside. Sometimes he moved too late to get out of the way, and sometimes he never moved at all.

I saw Hamilton's first pitch coming in and knew it was head high. But Tony didn't start to react until the last fraction of a second. Instinctively he threw up his hands to protect his head, but not nearly in time. The ball crashed into the side of his face with a sharp crack that I swear could have been heard clearly all over that noisy ballpark. It sounded like the ball hit his helmet, so my immediate reaction was relief that the ball had struck plastic instead of flesh. But the sound was probably his cheekbone breaking. In his desperate scramble to get out of the way of the ball, Tony had dislodged his helmet, and the ball struck him flush in the left side of his face, just below the eye socket. Tony went down like he'd been clothes-lined by an NFL cornerback and didn't move.

Except for umpire Bill Valentine and catcher Bob Rodgers, I was first on the scene. I didn't like what I saw. Tony's face was swelling up like there was somebody inside his skull blowing up a balloon. The first thing I thought was he was going to lose his left eye. Blood was pouring out of his nose. I didn't know what else to do, so I knelt down beside him, loosened his belt a little so he could breathe easier, and whispered into his ear that everything was going to be all right. By now the rest of the team had gathered around him, worried looks on all their faces. The crowd was hushed. Suddenly Tony's legs kicked, as if in a belated reaction to what had just happened. He started to regain consciousness, but not all the way. It was obvious he was seriously injured. The two trainers, Buddy LeRoux and California's Freddy Frederico, attended to him and tried to make him comfortable, but there wasn't much else they could do for him. After several minutes passed it became evident he wasn't going to shake this off, so someone called for a stretcher. Jim Lonborg, Joy Foy, and Mike Ryan—three of our biggest guys—gently lifted up Tony's inert body and placed it onto the stretcher. He was carried into the clubhouse where Dr. Tom Tierney, the club physician, was already waiting.

Tony became fully conscious in the trainer's room. "It hurts like hell," he told the doc. "I heard a hissing sound, and that was all."

"I thought I was going to die," he said later. "Death was constantly on my mind."

By now his bruised face was so swollen his left eye was completely shut. An ambulance arrived, and Tony was rushed across the Charles River to Sancta Maria Hospital in Cambridge, where a neurosurgeon, Dr. Joseph Dorsey, was waiting to examine him. The diagnosis was a shattered cheekbone. Doctors would have to wait until the swelling went down to determine if there was any permanent damage to his eye. Dr. Dorsey said that if the ball had struck Tony an inch higher and to the right, he might have been killed.

When the Fenway Park crowd saw Tony being taken away on a stretcher, the fans began booing Hamilton, who had stayed on the mound with his arms folded across his chest. Later Hamilton insisted he hadn't intentionally beaned Tony.

"I haven't hit anyone all year," he said, which was pretty much true. Tony was the first batter he'd hit since being traded to the Angels from the New York Mets in June. He had hit one batter while with the Mets. "I certainly wasn't throwing at him. I was just trying to get the ball over. Tony stands right on top of the plate. He hangs over the plate as much as anyone in the league." Which was also true.

Although our thoughts were with Tony, we had to finish the game. Throughout the remainder of the contest, whenever someone came back into the dugout he'd ask: "What's the word on Tony? Have you heard anything about Tony?"

I was the first batter to face Hamilton after Jose Tartabull went in to run for Tony. I'm sure most fans can't understand how it's possible to stand at the plate after you've seen something as terrible as what just happened to Tony and not imagine it's going to happen to you. One would think the batter's box is the last place on earth you'd want to be. I won't pretend it's easy, but as a professional ballplayer you have to learn to beat back fear and hit. If you can't, you'll never make it out of the lower minor leagues. If you play long enough, every batter will get hit in the head sooner or later. You just pray the ball doesn't do any lasting damage.

I got beaned three times during my career. Twice I took pitches off the top of my helmet and nothing happened. The third one hastened the end of my career. It happened seven years after Tony's beaning, in September of 1974. Luis Tiant was pitching for us and getting hit hard by the Milwaukee Brewers, and he got mad and hit one of their guys. So I knew I was going down when I came to bat. I accepted that as part of the game, and I never really minded it because the ball thrown at your head is usually the easiest one to see, so you can get out of the way. But this time it was a Sunday afternoon at Fenway, and the glare off the center-field bleachers was blinding. Jim Slaton started his wind-up, and that was the last time I saw the ball. I strode toward where I imagined the ball was going to be, and I heard the umpire yell: "Watch out!" I tried to duck out of the way, but I still had no idea where the ball was. It struck me right behind the left ear, below the helmet. That pitch put me out for the rest of the year, and when I retired in the spring of 1977 at the age of 33 I was still feeling its effects. Slaton's pitch caused inner-ear damage, and I had trouble focusing my eyes after that.

So it wasn't fear I was feeling when I stepped in against Jack Hamilton; it was rage. I was so mad I wanted to hit one out of the ballpark to get back at him. I nearly did. I belted a 420-foot triple into the center-field triangle to chase home Tartabull with the first run of the game and scored myself when shortstop Jim Fregosi mishandled the relay. I walked in the sixth inning and scored on a single by Bell, putting us ahead 3–0. Bell gave up a couple of solo homers to Jimmie Hall late in the game but finished with a four-hitter, and we hung on to win 3–2.

Hamilton tried to visit Tony in the hospital the next morning but was denied admittance to his room. Few visitors were allowed, although Mr. Yawkey was one of them. The press was barred from interviewing him, but a photographer was permitted to snap a photograph. It wasn't a pretty picture. There was a huge, ugly, shiny black bruise around his eye that was still swollen shut. The initial prognosis was that Tony would be disabled for three weeks.

He wouldn't play again for 18 months. The fracture healed, but there was a hole in his retina that could not be repaired. Tony missed the entire 1968 season and figured his baseball career was over. But his vision suddenly got better, and he made a miraculous comeback in 1969, playing 141 games and hitting .255 with 20 homers and 82 RBIs while being named the AL's Comeback Player of the Year. In 1970 it appeared he was back all the way as he enjoyed the best year of his career, hitting .266 with 36 homers and 116 RBIs.

But his vision began to deteriorate late in the season. The Red Sox, again concerned about his future, traded him to the Angels in October, and by the following spring Tony could barely see out of his left eye. Midway through the 1971 season, hitting a miserable .222 with only four homers and 15 RBIs in 74 games, he announced his retirement from baseball and virtually disappeared from public life.

Three years later his vision began to improve again, and Tony wanted to attempt another comeback. The Red Sox were skeptical but invited him to spring training in 1975. He was rusty and struggled. But a couple of encouraging games near the end of the exhibition season convinced the Red Sox to keep him, and he was the designated hitter on Opening Day at Fenway Park. When Conigliaro approached the plate for his first at-bat, a leggy, well dressed, attractive female admirer sashayed down from the grandstand into the box seats and tossed a bouquet of red roses onto the field. At the age of 30 Tony still had the looks, the charisma, and the personality. But his talent had eroded.

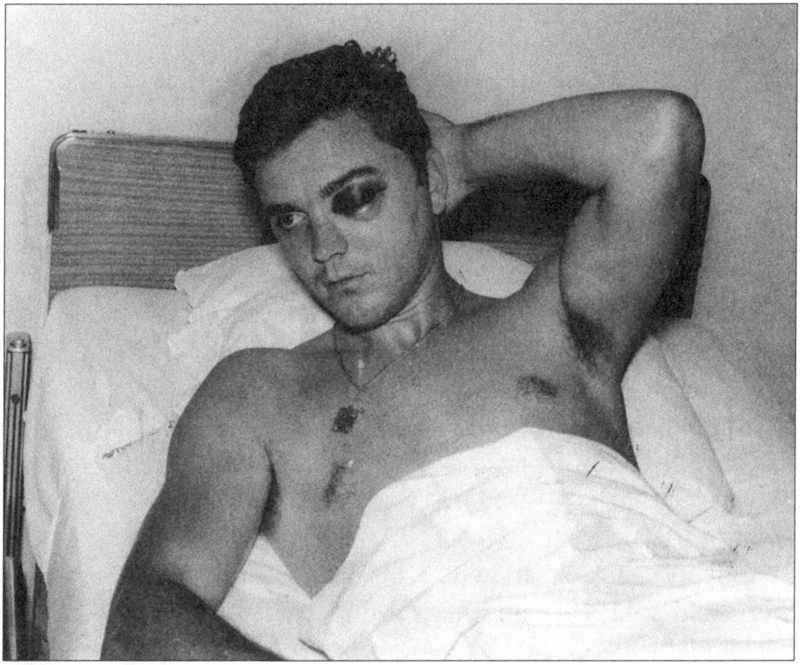

Handsome Tony Conigliaro rests in his hospital bed the day after being hit in the face by a Jack Hamilton pitch. It wasn't a pretty picture. (*Courtesy of the Boston Red Sox*)

The Red Sox kept him until mid-June, although he was barely playing by then. We were on our way to winning our first pennant since 1967, and the club could not afford to carry him any longer after we acquired second baseman Denny Doyle in a trade with the Angels. Tony was hitting .123 with two homers and nine RBIs in 21 games when the Red Sox asked him to go back to the minor leagues to try and resurrect his career. Tony C. declined and retired for good.

Tony moved out to San Francisco and became a sportscaster at a local TV station. On January 3, 1982, he flew to Boston to interview for a job as the analyst for Red Sox games on cable TV.

As his brother Billy was driving him back to Logan Airport, Tony told him he was confident he was going to get the job. While he was riding in the car he suffered a massive heart attack. Billy sped to Massachusetts General, the nearest hospital, but Tony was in a coma by the time they reached the emergency room. He never fully recovered and spent the remainder of his life in a nursing home in nearby Salem. On February 24, 1990, a year in which he might have been triumphantly entering the Hall of Fame except for that one pitch on a hot summer night back in 1967, Tony C. passed away. He was 45 years old.

WILD WEEKEND

With Tony C. watching the game on national TV from his hospital room through his one good eye, we had a slugfest with the Angels the following afternoon. We led by five runs going into the ninth, and it still came down to the final, nerve-wracking out.

The Angels struck for three runs in the first inning off Jose Santiago. George Scott hit a two-run homer in the bottom of the inning off Rickey Clark. We traded runs in the third and tied it in the fourth on a double by Mike Andrews. The Angels chased Santiago in the fifth and retook the lead, 6–4. We got a run back in the bottom of the inning, and then Carl Yastrzemski finally put us ahead 7–6 with a two-run homer off Jim Coates in the sixth. It looked like we were putting the game out of reach in the seventh against California's relief ace, Minnie Rojas. I singled, Elston Howard doubled, and Andrews was walked intentionally to load the bases. Dick Williams sent up Norm Siebern to pinch hit for John Wyatt, and he cleared the bases with a triple, making the score 10–6.

We picked up two insurance runs in the eighth that we never thought we'd need. Yaz led off with a double, his fourth hit of the game, and Boomer singled him to third. Howard hit a fly to left, and Rick Reichardt's throw beat Yaz to the plate. But Yaz kicked the mitt off catcher Bob Rodgers' hand, and the ball rolled away. Boomer, seeing the ball was loose, kept coming toward the plate. Pitcher Bill Kelso finally retrieved the ball and threw it to Rodgers, who hadn't had a chance to get his mitt. Rodgers tried to catch the ball with his bare hand and couldn't handle it as Boomer scored to up our lead to 12–7.

It wasn't over, though. Roger Repoz and Jimmie Hall belted homers off Darrell Brandon in the ninth, and all of a sudden it was 12–11. Williams brought in Jerry Stephenson, who had recently been called up from Toronto, and with such a shaky lead he even had Jim Lonborg warming up. Stephenson hit Reichardt with a pitch, and Moose Skowron singled him to third with two outs. The tying run was 90 feet away. Williams let Stephenson stay in the game, and Rodgers chopped a ball over the mound. I knew it was going to be a close play, even with a slow guy like Rodgers running. Either Andrews or I could have handled the ball, but Mike would have either needed to plant his feet before throwing or to make an awkward throw across his body, and there wasn't time for that. I cut in front of him, snared the ball, and with my momentum carrying me toward first was able to nail Rodgers by a half-step and end the game.

We finished the series with a doubleheader on Sunday in front of a packed house of 33,840 at Fenway. The first game was a laugher, our first one in five weeks. Switch-hitting Reggie Smith became the first player in Red Sox history to hit homers from both sides plate in the same game and drove in five runs. Yaz clouted his 30th homer of the season, and I also connected. We won 12–2, but after scoring 12 runs the day before and barely hanging on, we were a little apprehensive until this one was over. And with good reason. It turned out the Angels were just a wee tardy busting out.

The Angels erupted for six runs against Dave Morehead in the second inning of the nightcap and tacked on two more in the fourth off Dan Osinski to grab an 8–0 lead. But we refused to pack it in, even with All-Star Jim McGlothlin pitching for the Angels, and began chipping away at the huge deficit. Smith smacked his third homer of the day in the bottom of the inning, and Yaz socked a three-run homer in the fifth, chopping California's lead in half. By then I was already on the bench. With the score so lopsided and my wrist still aching, Williams thought it was a good time to give me a little break.

In the sixth we loaded the bases on walks to Andrews and Mike Ryan sandwiched around a pinch double by Joe Foy off Jack Hamilton. California manager Bill Rigney brought in Minnie Rojas, the league's top reliever that year, to face Dalton Jones, who greeted him with a two-run double off the center-field wall. Jose Tartabull hit a sacrifice fly, and then Jerry Adair tied the game at 8–8 with a single. Every Red Sox fan old enough to remember can recall what happened after that. Adair lofted a dramatic home run into the left-field screen off Rojas in the eighth, completing our fantastic comeback and putting us ahead 9–8. What most of the fans probably don't remember is that the Angels had runners at second and third with nobody out in the ninth after Don Mincher singled and Reichardt doubled.

By then Williams was out of the game, too. Rojas hit Yaz in the elbow right after Adair's homer, and with Conigliaro's beaning fresh and vivid in our minds, Dick went ballistic. He was subdued at first, checking with Yaz to make sure he was okay. Yaz said he was. But as soon as Dick got back to the dugout, he yelled out at Yaz: "Cut somebody open! When you go into second, go in spikes high, and you'd better cut somebody up!" He wanted the Angels to hear him.

He wanted them to know they weren't going to intimidate the Red Sox. The problem was the umpires could hear him, too. Bill Valentine, who was umpiring at first base, yelled back at Williams: "Cut it out!"

Williams, enraged, bolted back out of the dugout to confront Valentine. "What's all this about hitting someone?" Valentine demanded. "How many has Lonborg hit? Nineteen or so?" After Williams put in his two cents, he spit. Valentine said Dick spit on his shoes, so he threw him out of the game. Williams insisted he had spat on the ground.

So Eddie Popowski was nominally managing the team in the ninth when the Angels rallied, although Dick was camped in the shadows of the runway to the clubhouse, dictating strategy. Pop waved the infield in, a big gamble with the potential winning run already in scoring position at second base. If a ground ball got between the infielders, we might very well lose this game. But Jose Santiago, pitching in relief only 24 hours after getting shelled in his Saturday start, got Rodgers to ground to second as the runners held and fanned Bobby Knoop for the second out. Tom Satriano was walked intentionally to load the bases and bring Rojas to the plate, and Rigney countered by sending up the scary Skowron and his 211 career homers to pinch hit. With the infield now back, Skowron bounced a ball into the hole at shortstop. Everyone in the park held their breath. But Adair got there, backhanded the ball, and made an off-balance throw to Andrews covering second just in the nick of time for the game-ending force. We had swept the four-game series and were back in third place, only 1½ games behind the first-place Minnesota Twins.

UNSUNG HEROES

After the California series we ran our winning streak to eight games against the Washington Senators. The bench that Dick

O'Connell had put together for Dick Williams continued to pay huge dividends. The first game was tied 5–5 in the ninth when Jerry Adair doubled and scored the winning run on a single by Elston Howard. We swept a doubleheader the next night. Jerry Stephenson dueled Washington's Phil Ortega, who had won eight in a row, for 6 ½ scoreless innings until Dalton Jones broke it up with a two-run triple. We led 2–1 in the ninth when the Senators loaded the bases against John Wyatt with nobody out. Adair, playing second, grabbed a grounder and threw home for one out, and Howard fired the ball down to first to complete a double play. Wyatt polished off the save with a strikeout. Gary Bell won the nightcap 5–3, his eighth win since joining us in early June, and we moved into second place and pulled within one point of the White Sox, who were back on top.

The Senators ended our winning streak with a 3–2 victory on August 23, but we rebounded to win the finale of the five-game series 7–5 as Adair, Howard, and newcomer Jim Landis all homered. Landis, a veteran outfielder recently released by Detroit whom O'Connell had picked up to replace Conigliaro on the roster, had to fight the brutal late-afternoon sun in Fenway Park's right field before catching a ball for the final out with the bases loaded. We won 10 of 12 on the homestand and flew to Chicago to play the White Sox, who were still just one point ahead of us in the standings, in a five-game showdown at Comiskey Park.

THE HAWK

Many baseball historians will tell you that Catfish Hunter became the first high-priced free agent after Oakland Athletics owner Charlie Finley failed to deposit the deferred half of the pitcher's $100,000 salary into a life insurance fund in 1974. The case went to arbitration, and Catfish was declared a free agent by arbitrator Peter Seitz. Free to sign with the team of his choice, Catfish

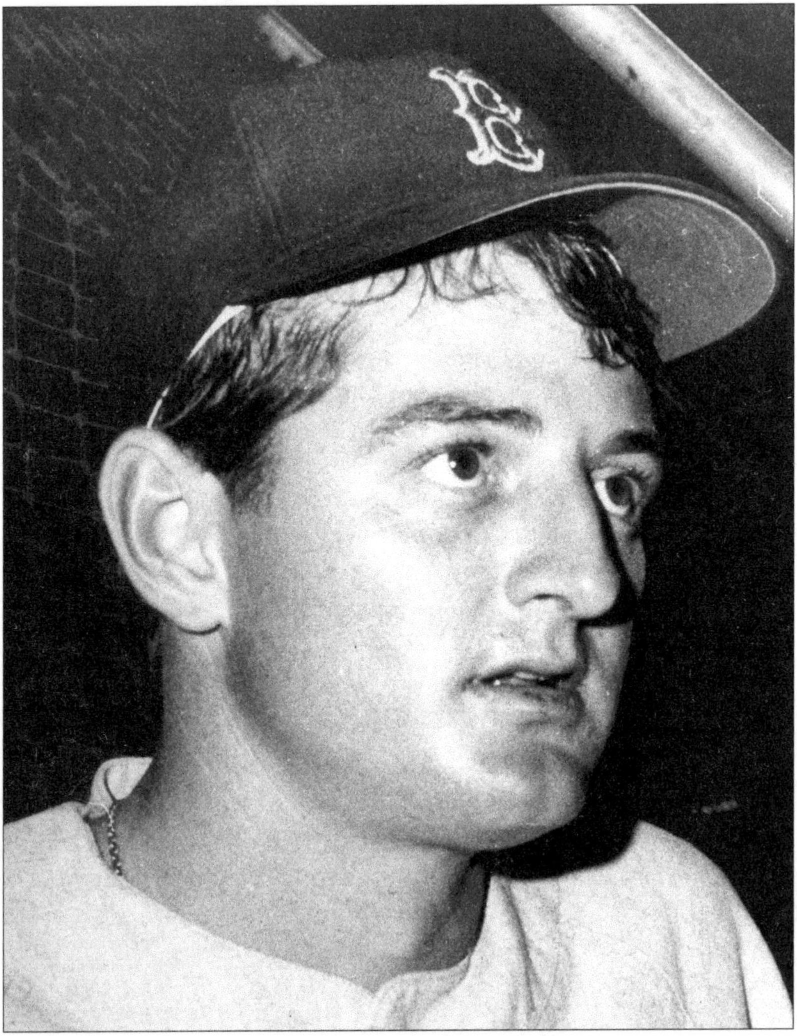

Ken "Hawk" Harrelson signed the first lucrative free-agent contract in baseball history and replaced injured Tony Conigliaro in right field. Hawk quickly became one of the most popular players on the Red Sox. (*Courtesy of the Boston Red Sox*)

accepted a five-year deal with the New York Yankees for $3.5 million in 1975. Hunter's deal would set the standard for all free agents when the century-old reserve clause that had bound players to their teams for life was struck down by Seitz a year later. But seven years before Catfish, a fit thrown by Finley had enabled Ken "Hawk" Harrelson to become baseball's first true expensive free agent.

After we had taken three of four games from the Athletics in Boston in early August, pitcher Lew Krausse had gotten drunk on the TWA flight back to Kansas City and caused quite a commotion. When Finley learned of the incident a few days later, he suspended him indefinitely for "conduct unbecoming a major-league player." A penitent Krausse accepted the suspension, but the rest of the team was up in arms. The players were certain Finley had a spy in their midst, and they issued a public statement accusing the owner of undermining the club's morale by using informers. When manager Alvin Dark called the statement "the most courageous thing I have ever seen," Finley fired him on August 20 and demanded the players retract the statement. They refused, and the dismissal of Dark, a religious man whom they all liked and respected, merely fueled their anger. Harrelson was the most vocal of the rebels and allegedly called Finley "a menace to baseball."

When Finley read that comment in the papers, he angrily phoned Harrelson in his hotel room in Baltimore, where the Athletics were playing. Hawk, who had always had a good relationship with Finley, told him he'd been misquoted, that he'd never used the word "menace" and promised to say so publicly. But Hawk also bluntly told him his recent actions had been "bad for baseball." The furious Finley told Harrelson he was finished and released him outright, making him an unrestricted free agent.

Harrelson was not a superstar in 1967. Nor was he the typical washed-up player in his mid- or late 30s who'd been released because he couldn't play anymore. Hawk was only 25 years old and just entering the prime years of his career. His services would be very much in demand on the open market.

Kenneth Smith Harrelson had been born in South Carolina in 1941 and raised in Savannah by his mother, who went to work to support him when he was 10. She enrolled him in a military school where he starred in football, basketball, baseball, and golf. The University of Georgia offered him a basketball scholarship, but he was also being courted by seven major-league teams and chose to sign with Kansas City in 1959. Harrelson displayed good power in the minors and had a monster year for Binghamton in the Class AA Eastern League in 1962, hitting .272 with 38 homers and 138 RBIs. After hitting .300 with nine homers and 31 RBIs in 41 games for Class AAA Portland in 1963, he was called up to the A's.

Harrelson did not hit for much of an average in the majors but was beginning to develop into a slugger by 1965 when he socked 23 homers and drove in 66 runs. The Athletics traded him to Washington for pitcher Jim Duckworth midway through the 1966 season and then reacquired him a year later in a straight cash deal.

Hawk had been hitting .305 with six homers and 30 RBIs in 61 games since returning to Kansas City in June when Finley cut him loose.

I didn't know much about the Hawk other than he had a big beak that had earned him his nickname, he was loaded with charisma, and he was one of the few K.C. players willing to ride the mule Finley kept at the ballpark as a mascot. I'd heard he was a heckuva golfer, a pool shark, and unbeatable in arm wrestling. I knew that as a ballplayer he was a weak defensive first baseman and even worse in the outfield, but the guys on the Red Sox who had played with him in Kansas City all said he could hit. "Hees a goood guy, a preety goood heeter," Jose Tartabull told us. Hawk certainly seemed to kill us every time we had played the A's or the

Senators. Less than three weeks earlier Harrelson had homered, doubled, and driven in three runs to beat us 8–6 in a game at Fenway.

The bidding for his services became intense. Seven teams wanted him, including the White Sox, who were desperate for someone with punch. They offered him $100,000 to sign . . . and this was in an era when the average major-league salary was $19,000 a year. Hawk mulled the offers for a few days. On August 25 he decided to pass up the offer from the White Sox and sign a contract with the Red Sox that would extend through the 1968 season and pay him $80,000, a figure that broke down to more than $11,000 a month during the playing season. Not bad for someone who was making $12,500 a year in Kansas City and was $20,000 in debt because of his flamboyant lifestyle. "This is the first time in my life," Hawk said, "I won't have to run down to the bank tomorrow and try somehow to get my checks covered." He was actually making more money now than Yaz, but nobody, including Yaz, cared. The only thing we cared about was whether or not he could catch the ball in the outfield, drive in some runs, and help us win the pennant.

If Charlie Finley thought he had made Harrelson a baseball pariah and driven him out of the game, he was absolutely wrong. "I'm sure he regrets it, but I don't care, even though he treated me well," Harrelson said. "The Red Sox are in the pennant fight, and I think we're going to win it."

Harrelson's signing drew a mixed reaction from the Boston press. "In Harrelson the Sox now have an even better golfer than Billy Herman," snidely wrote columnist Harold Kaese in the *Globe*. "But as a first baseman he is only slightly better than Zeke Bonura, and as an outfielder he has been more of a menace to pitchers than he said Charles Finley was to baseball."

As it turned out, Ken Harrelson and the Red Sox were an absolutely perfect fit. As soon as he joined us, we felt like we had known him all our lives. Jim Landis, who had been with us only a few days but long enough to help us win an important ballgame, was released to make room for him, and the Hawk filled the void left by Tony Conigliaro and helped us win the pennant. With his long hair, affinity for the latest and most outrageous fashions, and charisma, he became a cult figure in Boston.

A CHI-TOWN SHOWDOWN

The Brat, Eddie Stanky, was his usual impetuous self when we arrived in Chicago to play the light-hitting but pitching-rich White Sox for first place on Friday, August 25.

"We don't belong in the same league with Boston and all of those hairy-chested players and their new-breed manager," Stanky rambled, pretending to be in awe of us. "We're last in home runs, last in double plays, last in hitting. But we're in first place in the standings, and we're first in guts and determination, too. My boys are making a laughingstock out of the American League. It embarrasses the other teams to pick up the paper and see the White Sox in first place. The City of Culture is crying about Conigliaro's injury. Big deal. We've had injuries all season, but we aren't crying. Tonight Lonborg probably won't last through four innings."

By now we had become accustomed to Stanky's rants, and they went in one ear and out the other. To be taken so seriously after so many years of being insignificant had been a new and somewhat disconcerting experience for us earlier in the season, and initially we weren't sure how to respond to all the attention we were getting. But we were confident of our abilities now. Dick Williams had hardened us. We weren't going to be psyched out. The 100–1 shot Red Sox were not a fluke, and the Red Sox were not going to fold down the stretch.

Lonborg throttled the White Sox with a seven-hitter for his 17th victory and shut them out until the ninth inning. We banged out 16 hits—four of them by George Scott and three by Carl Yastrzemski, who also walked and scored three runs as he continued to tuck it to the Brat—and we won the first game of a twi-night doubleheader 7–1. We might have won the nightcap, too, if I had run the bases better.

I was on second base with one out in the seventh inning when Dalton Jones, pinch hitting for Mike Ryan, blooped a ball behind third base. Eddie Popowski, coaching third, was waving frantically for me to score. But I had a feeling the ball might be caught and played it safe. It fell in for a single, and I only got as far as third. Norm Siebern, pinch hitting for Lee Stange, hit a nubber in front of the plate. Had I broken for the plate immediately, as I should have done with one out, I probably would have scored. But I hesitated, and I was cut down. Williams gave me a stern lecture, reminding me I should know ahead of time what I'm going to do when I'm running the bases. We lost the game 2–1. At least Stange didn't get tagged with the loss this time; John Wyatt did when Ken Berry singled home the winning run in the eighth. "Stinger" was our hard-luck pitcher that summer. He routinely held teams to one or two runs, but we just couldn't score when he was pitching.

The split of the doubleheader knocked both teams out of first place. Dean Chance, who had thrown a rain-shortened five-inning perfect game against us a couple weeks earlier, hurled a no-hitter against Cleveland that vaulted the Twins into first place by a half-game.

Jerry Stephenson flirted with a no-hitter for five innings the next afternoon, and we rebounded to beat the White Sox 6–2. The Twins lost to Cleveland, and we were back in first place by half a game over Minnesota.

The series concluded with another doubleheader on Sunday. Yaz swatted a pair of homers in the first game, and we led 4–3 going into the bottom of the ninth. Berry, Chicago's fastest player, led off with a double and was bunted over to third. Duane Josephson hit a fly to right field that wasn't especially deep, but Jose Tartabull had a terrible throwing arm—he hadn't thrown out a runner on the bases all year—and I was instantly resigned to the notion that it would be a sacrifice fly and the game would be tied. But Tartabull got rid of the ball as quickly as humanly possible and put everything he had in his wispy little body behind the throw as Berry streaked for the plate, and now I thought Tartabull just might throw him out. Then, incredibly defying the laws of physics regarding force and gravity, Tartabull's throw was high, and Elston Howard had to leap for it. As soon as I saw Ellie leave his feet, I thought for sure Berry was going to be safe. Even more incredibly, Ellie leaped just high enough to grab the ball and get his left foot back down in time to block the sliding Berry from the plate. Berry spun around and reached for the plate with his hand, but down came Ellie's sweeping mitt to tag him on the hand before it could get there. My first reaction was: "Holy Jeez! A miracle!" It was a double play, the game was over, and we were still in first place. It was exactly the type of smart play we had expected from Howard when we obtained him from the Yankees on waivers in early August.

"At the end of the season," Harold Kaese prophetically wrote in the *Boston Globe* the next morning, "Howard's left foot may go down in baseball history as the first left foot ever to have won a pennant for the Red Sox."

Howard was deeply satisfied to have made that crucial play against Stanky's team. "I've never hated many people in this game," he said, "but I don't want any part of that runt."

The nightcap was dramatic yet anti-climactic. Jose Santiago threw 9 ⅔ shutout innings at the White Sox before leaving with a shoulder injury after running into Mike Ryan when they both went after a bunt, but we couldn't score either. Chicago won it 1–0 in the 11th when Darrell Brandon walked four batters, including

Rocky Colavito with the bases loaded. Gary Peters, beaten by Lonborg on Friday night, pitched all 11 innings for the White Sox. We won the series but fell to second, one point behind the Twins.

EXHAUSTION

The challenge of a 162-game baseball season isn't really physical. While they sometimes may not look it, ballplayers are generally well conditioned. While some guys like George Scott and Joe Foy constantly battle to keep their weight down, and bumps, bruises, and abrasions never get enough time to properly heal, it's the mental part of the game that wears down a player by late summer. Physically we can go a lot longer than we think we can, because it's your mind that gets tired first. The positioning of the constellations isn't the only reason they're called the dog days. Staving off mental exhaustion is the biggest challenge for a ballplayer because you can never take enough time off to let your mind get refreshed. So you play through it. And in 1967 we discovered that in the heat of a pennant race, the rush of adrenaline helps you get through it easier than when you're 25 games out and marking time until the season ends.

We finished the road trip in New York, and as if we weren't dragging already, having been mentally drained by too many close, pressure-packed games, we had to play 29 innings in one night against the Yankees on August 29. That night all but emptied our adrenaline reserves.

We had shut out the ninth-place Yankees 3–0 behind Dave Morehead and Sparky Lyle the previous night, an evening during which Carl Yastrzemski, a Long Island native, was honored by the fans and had 100 relatives and friends in attendance. Half the crowd of 27,296 seemed to be made up of Red Sox rooters who had also come down from New England to watch us play. Now, in the first game of a twi-nighter, Jim Lonborg beat the Yankees 2–1 for his 18th victory, helping win his own game with an RBI single. The nightcap went 20 innings and took six hours and 15 minutes to play, ending just a couple of minutes before 2 a.m. This marathon was incredibly tense and frustrating, and we lost it 4–3. In the fourth inning Yaz had thrown out Steve Whitaker trying for an inside-the-park homer. Some five hours later, after we had lost, a weary Yaz grumbled: "If I'd known how the damned thing was going to turn out, I'd have thrown that ball into the stands." By then, we all wished he had, too.

Ken Harrelson had joined us in New York and homered in his first at-bat in a Red Sox uniform, putting us up 2–0 in the second inning. But those were the only runs we got for the next couple of hours. The game was tied 2–2 after 10. I doubled in the 11th, and Siebern singled me home to put us ahead, but Whitaker hit one out of the park against Lyle in the bottom of the inning to keep it going. Yaz and Reggie Smith made sensational catches with two on in the 15th to prolong the affair. But the Yankees finally won it in the 20th on a single by Horace Clarke.

Despite the loss, we moved into first place by a half-game over the Twins. But there would be no rest for the weary. Less than 12 hours later we were back at Yankee Stadium for the final game of the series. We were all whacked, but Yaz was in an 0-for-18 slump, and Dick Williams decided to give him the day off. Williams asked me if I needed a day off, too. I felt like I was about to evaporate, but I told him I could play. I don't want to come off sounding like some kind of hero, but with Yaz getting the day off I didn't think we should be playing without two of our regulars.

"How do you feel?" Williams asked Yaz when he wandered into the dugout shortly before the start of the game.

"I can play a little defense and pinch hit," Yaz offered.

"Well, sit down and rest," Williams said.

We played like zombies. Lefty Al Downing mowed us down, striking out 10 in the first nine innings. Again we went into extra innings, tied 1–1. Williams put a restless Yaz into the game in the eighth, and he won it for us in the 11th by hitting a homer off Downing. It was his 35th homer of the season, giving him the AL lead in that department. Yaz was also leading the league with 95 runs batted in and was second in hitting at .311.

The 2–1 triumph put us ahead in the race by 1 ½ games, which would be our largest lead of the season. But after having played 49 innings in three days, we were all too exhausted to celebrate. And even though we were going home to Boston, we knew things weren't going to get any easier, because the White Sox were coming to town for four more games.

8

SEPTEMBER 1967

Exhausted from our ordeal in New York, we just couldn't get it together against the Chicago White Sox and lost three of the four games, costing us first place. Ken Harrelson was the show in the only game we won, a 10–2 rout on September 1 in front of an SRO crowd of 34,054. Prior to the game Hawk, whose preferred position was first base, worked an extra 15 minutes trying to get accustomed to playing right field.

"For the first time I was hoping they'd hit flyballs to me," he said after the workout. "The other day I was scared to death out there."

But his first fly that night was a misadventure. He caught it . . . eventually. But Tommy Agee, who had been on first, embarrassed him by taking second on the play. The White Sox kept testing him throughout the game, but he caught everything and finished with seven putouts. Some nights it was going to look like the Barnum & Bailey Circus out in right field. But Hawk worked at his defense, and over time it got better.

Harrelson also worked the White Sox over with his bat. He doubled, tripled, and homered, drove in four runs, scored three, and came within a single of hitting for the cycle. The bleacher crowd in right field gave him a standing ovation after every hit, and from that day on Hawk Harrelson could do no wrong in the eyes of Red Sox fans. He was hoping to get one more at-bat in the eighth to get the single that would complete his cycle and, with Dick Williams' permission since we were so far ahead, he intended to stop at first base no matter how far he hit the ball. He had hit for the cycle a couple of times in the minors but never in the majors. But he didn't get up again.

With the club in second place, a half-game behind Minnesota after the Chicago series, Williams needed a little levity and got it from an old teammate from the Gold Sox years. Dick Stuart, who was playing in Japan, sent a letter that broke up our gruff manager as he read it. "I see in the papers that come here once in a while that Yaz has a chance to lead the league in all three departments," Big Stu wrote. "I led the league once in all three, too. A) most errors B) most strikeouts C) best quotes to the press."

A PROMISE KEPT

We won two of three from the Senators in Washington, then returned to Fenway and took three of four from the Yankees. Our 9–1 romp over the Yanks on September 10 was our 82nd victory of the season, assuring us of a winning record for the first time since 1958 and fulfilling Dick Williams' spring training promise that we'd win more than we'd lose.

"I feel pleased. Quite pleased," he said. "That's pretty good for a club that was in ninth place, a half-game out of the basement, a year ago. That's a lot of ground to make up."

When we reached that mark we felt really good. By then, however, it wasn't our goal anymore. Now there was a pennant to be won. We had a chance to play in the World Series, and wouldn't that be something? But most of us had never experienced a pennant race before, and we were starting to feel the pressure. With three other teams still in the hunt, you felt like you had to win every night because at least one of the other three teams was probably going to.

"The season seemed to shoot by," Yaz reflected. "When I think there are only 17 games left I almost panic. You can't lose and say, 'We'll get 'em tomorrow,' anymore. You feel that you must win every game."

That kind of pressure was fun, though, especially for a young team that no one really expected to win. I think that after you get older the pressure is exponentially greater because you're either nearing the end of your career and know you may never get another shot, or because you're playing for a veteran team that is expected to win. I felt the pressure much more in 1975 when I was 32 and we had already won a pennant and been a contender for eight years than in 1967 when I was 24.

For the guys who had come up through the Red Sox system, 1967 was the first time we had ever engaged in the pastime of scoreboard watching. Any game involving Minnesota, Chicago, or Detroit was of paramount interest to us. In those days the guy from the grounds crew assigned to operating the mechanical scoreboard from inside the Green Monster only updated the scores of the out-of-town games after each full inning. But he knew the half-inning scores because they were also phoned down to him from the press box as they came over the ticker. During lulls in the action, Yaz would sidle up to the scoreboard and through one of the slots ask the guy what the latest scores were. Then Yaz would pass them on to the rest of us.

Those guys who worked inside the Monster had a flair for the dramatic. They knew everyone at Fenway Park was watching the game with one eye on the scoreboard, and when the team playing the Tigers, Twins, or White Sox would forge ahead, they'd pull the old number out of the slot and leave it empty for a few tantalizing seconds. A hush would fall over the crowd while they waited anxiously for the new number to be inserted. Had the Senators pulled within a run of the Tigers, tied it up, or gone ahead? The operator would finally drop a number into the slot that showed the Senators had just gone ahead by two runs, and the place would go bananas.

LONBORG WINS 20

Jim Lonborg earned his 20th victory of the season on September 12, outdueling Catfish Hunter to beat Kansas City 3–1. Lonnie's win pulled us into a first-place tie with the Twins, who were edged 5–4 by Washington.

It didn't come easy. Lonnie had to pitch his way out of one jam after another. The Athletics had a runner on third with one out in the second but couldn't score. In the third Bert Campaneris tried to sneak home from third on the front end of a double steal. Mike Ryan had a prearranged signal to alert Lonnie that the ball would be thrown directly back to him instead of second if Campy tried it, and when he did they executed it perfectly. Lonnie next pitched out of a bases-loaded, no-out predicament in the fourth. We also turned four double plays behind him.

Reggie Smith staked him to a 1–0 lead with a homer in the fifth, but Campy tied it up with a homer in the eighth. Ryan led off the bottom of the inning with a single, and Jose Tartabull pinch ran. Lonborg got the bunt sign from Eddie Popowski. But when Lonnie saw Sal Bando charging hard from third base, he pulled his top hand down the handle and swung away.

"Dick has told me—and I think a lot of the pitchers—that if the fielders really charge, we have the option of swinging away even if the bunt sign is on," he explained. "I could see the third baseman coming in, so I just faked the bunt and tried to hit it past him to left field."

Lonnie's aim wasn't very good. Instead he lined the ball into right-center for a triple to chase home Tartabull with the winning run and scored himself moments later on a sacrifice fly by Mike Andrews.

We swept the two-game series with a 4–2 win over the Athletics the next afternoon. A's pitchers twice intentionally walked Hawk Harrelson, their former teammate, to get to me. I delivered an RBI single the first time and a two-run double the next.

But the Baltimore Orioles came to town and swept a three-game series from us. We were extremely fortunate that all the other contenders had bad weekends. We had dropped to third place but were only a game behind the first-place Tigers, and we were going to Detroit to play them.

A ONE-MAN DALTON GANG

As if Dick Williams needed a reminder, a Red Sox fan from Indiana sent him a telegram in Detroit on September 18. "Remember Dalton Jones hits a ton at Tiger Stadium."

Williams knew that, of course, and started Jones at third base. My roomie delivered three singles in his first four at-bats, but we went into the ninth inning trailing 5–4. The Tigers had entrusted the lead to a submarining rookie named Fred Lasher. Lasher had not given up a home run all season in 93 innings split between the minors and Detroit. But two outs away from saving a victory, Yaz slammed one of his pitches into the upper deck in right field for his 40th homer, tying the score at 5–5. In the 10th Jones planted a Mike Marshall pitch in the upper deck for his fourth hit of the game, and we pulled out a 6–5 win that created a three-way deadlock for first place between us, Detroit, and Minnesota with Chicago only a half-game back. Jones now boasted 18 career homers, six of which had been struck in Tiger Stadium and three of which had been game-winners.

Utility infielder Dalton Jones (left) and I were roommates on the road. If Dalton could have played every game of his career in Tiger Stadium, he would have made the Hall of Fame. (*Courtesy of the Boston Red Sox*)

"There's something about this place," Jones mused, sounding mystical. "I just feel better coming to the plate here than I do anywhere else."

Yaz, who had three hits in the game, finally overhauled Baltimore's Frank Robinson for the batting lead and now led the league in all three Triple Crown categories with a .314 average, 40 homers, and 107 RBIs.

THE DRAMA CLUB

That was the first of three straight games we dramatically won in our last at-bat. The Tigers took a 2–1 lead into the ninth the next night but should have had a bigger cushion. They had the bases loaded in the third only to see Lee Stange escape the jam by getting Jerry Lumpe to ground into a double play. The Tigers loaded the bases with nobody out in the eighth but couldn't score when Jose Santiago got Norm Cash to foul out and Bill Freehan to rap into a double play.

Mickey Lolich had held us to four hits over the first eight innings. But Jerry Adair led off the ninth with a single and Yaz walked. George Scott singled home pinch runner Jose Tartabull and the game was tied. Detroit manager Mayo Smith waved in an old friend, 21-game winner Earl Wilson, from the bullpen for his first relief appearance of the season. Reggie Smith bunted the runners along and Williams sent up Dalton Jones to hit for Hawk Harrelson. This time the Tigers took no chances with Jones, walking him intentionally to fill the bases and get to me. Williams called me back and summoned left-handed-hitting Norm Siebern to pinch hit. Wilson uncorked a wild pitch, and Yaz raced home with the go-ahead run. After Siebern was passed intentionally, catcher Russ Gibson hit a sacrifice fly to put us ahead 4–2.

The drama was far from over, however. After all the maneuvering in the top of the inning, we didn't exactly have our best defense on the diamond to try to preserve the lead. Boomer was at third, Andrews was at short, Siebern was playing first, and Tartabull was in right field. Fortunately, Don Wert led off the bottom of the ninth by hitting the ball to the right guy, and Yaz made a sliding catch to rob him of a hit. Santiago walked the next two batters, and when Mayo Smith sent up left-handed-hitting future Hall of Famer Eddie Mathews—whom the Tigers had picked up in mid-August for the stretch drive—and his 508 career homers to pinch hit for weak-hitting Ray Oyler, Williams was in a bind. He'd used Sparky Lyle earlier in the game, and rookie Bill Landis was the only southpaw reliever left in the pen. Williams had only used him for 29 innings all season, and he hadn't pitched at all in three weeks.

Landis was another one of our many refugees from the Kansas City organization. Dick O'Connell had drafted him off the roster of Class AAA Vancouver, where he had compiled an 11–10 record with a 3.40 ERA in 1966. Williams kept him on the roster but didn't have a lot of faith in him after his Red Sox debut against the Yankees back in April. He walked the first two batters, and Williams scrambled out and dressed him down.

"He told me in his gentle way," Landis recalled, "that if I didn't throw strikes he was going to send me so far down in the minors that I wouldn't ever get out of his doghouse."

When Landis walked the next batter, a disgusted Williams came back out to remove him from the game. "That was my first trip to his doghouse," Landis said. "The next time I pitched was 28 days later."

Now Williams had no other real option except to use him. As he was leaving the bullpen, Landis asked the veteran Gary Bell for some advice. Could he get Mathews out with low fastballs? Bell had no idea; he'd spent his entire career in the American League while Mathews had spent his in the National.

"I told him yes to make him feel good," Bell related afterward. "But, heck, I didn't know what got him out."

Williams was waiting on the mound with the ball when Landis arrived. "Do you know what that thing is there?" he inquired, pointing to the white slab in center of the mound.

"Yeah. It's the rubber," Landis replied.

"I knew then he was all right," Williams said.

Landis struck out Mathews swinging at a low fastball, and Bell came on to face Al Kaline. As part of a pitcher's routine, Bell looked around to check the defense before delivering his first pitch.

"When I went down for the rosin bag and saw who was there at third and short with Kaline up, I nearly choked!" Bell quipped. Kaline lined out to center to end the game, knocking the Tigers out of their share of first place and leaving us tied with the Twins.

We left Detroit and headed to Cleveland, where we staged another ninth-inning rally to win the game. Lonborg was pitching on short rest now—he would start six of the last 17 games of the season—and wasn't particularly sharp. Yaz homered in the sixth off fireballer "Sudden" Sam McDowell, I added a two-run shot later in the inning to put us ahead 3–2, and Andrews hit one out in the seventh. But Tony Horton, another old friend, and Max Alvis swatted back-to-back homers off Lonnie in the bottom of the seventh, and the game was tied 4–4 going into the ninth.

With two outs and nobody on, Yaz drilled a single off George Culver for his fourth hit of the game and went to second on a wild pitch. Culver pitched carefully to Boomer, who was among the league's leading hitters with a .301 average, and walked him. Reggie Smith then lashed an 0-and-2 pitch to right to score Yaz with the winning run.

We didn't need a ninth-inning rally to beat the Indians the next night, but we did have to hang on for dear life after blowing most of a 6–1 lead before winning 6–5.

Our final road series of the year was in Baltimore, and the Orioles walloped us 10–0 in the first game of a twi-night doubleheader. We fell behind 2–0 in the nightcap but roared back and won 10–3. The Orioles jumped out to a 4–0 lead the following day. We came back to take a 5–4 lead on a two-run homer by Yaz but couldn't hold it and lost 7–5. We earned a split of the series by beating the Orioles 11–7 on September 24 for our 90th victory as Dalton Jones had four hits and five RBIs and George Scott and Jerry Adair also had four hits each. We were in second place, a half-game behind Minnesota while Chicago was one game back and Detroit 1½, and we were coming home for the final week of the season.

FLIRTING WITH DISASTER

We were gladdened by the presence of Tony Conigliaro that final week. He was still on the disabled list but was in uniform and on the bench, wearing sunglasses to protect his damaged left eye.

We grabbed a share of first place without even playing on September 25. While we had the day off, the Twins were clobbered 9–2 by the California Angels. With the seventh-place Indians coming to town for a pair of games, we were supremely confident the pennant would be decided when we played Minnesota on the weekend. With luck we might only have to beat the Twins once.

People kept telling us: "You can't look past the Indians! You can't look past the Indians!" But we did. All we had on our minds was Minnesota. Cleveland jumped out to a 6–0 lead against us the next day. Yaz tried to get us back into it with a three-run homer, his 43rd, tying Ted Williams' club record for homers by a left-handed hitter, but we lost 6–3 while the Twins were beating California 7–3 to take over sole possession of first. Luis Tiant pitched for the Indians and kept taunting us throughout the game. "Tight asses! You guys have tight asses!" And then you'd hear that squeaky little laugh of his.

Our situation became even bleaker the next day. Lonborg was pitching on two days' rest. The Indians lit him up for four runs in the second, and we lost 6–0. We caught a small break when the Angels beat the Twins 5–1, keeping us a game behind Minnesota. But the White Sox, who also began the day one game behind, were playing the last-place Athletics in a doubleheader and would almost certainly be in first place by the end of the evening. Chicago would then finish out the season with another weak club, the Washington Senators, while we and the Twins were trying to knock each other out, and Detroit was engaged in a tough four-game series with a good California team. But the White Sox must have made the same miscalculation we did and got caught looking past the A's, who shocked them by winning both games 5–2 and 4–0.

"I thought we were dead. Not only dead but buried," Yaz said. "When I heard that Chicago lost twice to Kansas City, I almost couldn't believe it. The whole thing is incredible! Here we are with another great chance to win the pennant, and we really don't deserve it. We've just got to be the luckiest team in baseball. Maybe we are destined to win this thing like people say."

We had two days off to prepare for the Twins. Meanwhile, the White Sox turned it into a three-team race by eliminating themselves with a 1–0 loss to the Senators on Friday, September 29. By virtue of playing each other, either we or the Twins were going to finish the schedule with 92 victories. Chicago now could not win more than 91. Detroit, meanwhile, had to play back-to-back doubleheaders with the Angels at Tiger Stadium. If the Tigers swept them while we split our series with the Twins, or won three out of four if we beat the Twins twice, Detroit would win the pennant.

THE MVP

Over the final 10 games of the season, Carl Yastrzemski played like a dervish. Even if he hadn't done a thing all season to help us win, Yaz would have deserved the Most Valuable Player Award based on those last 10 games alone.

"When I go to the plate now, I'm thinking of only one thing: I try to hit every pitch out of the ballpark," he said in mid-September. "Put it this way: I'm going down swinging. If a pitcher gets me out, I'll tip my cap to him."

This was a scene we saw 44 times in 1967, Carl Yastrzemski shaking third-base coach Eddie Popowski's hand as he rounded the bases after hitting another home run. (*Courtesy of the Boston Red Sox*)

Yaz didn't do much cap-tipping over those 10 games. He hit .541 and slugged .946, going 20-for-37 with four homers, three doubles, 14 runs batted in, and 11 runs scored. Here's his game-by-game performance for the eight games leading up to the final weekend:

September 20—Yaz goes 4-for-5, hitting a homer off Cleveland left-hander Sam McDowell in the sixth and then scoring the winning run in the ninth after singling. The Red Sox win 5–4.

September 21—Yaz goes 1-for-4 with a walk and scores a run in a 6–5 win over the Indians.

September 22—Yaz goes 1-for-3 with a walk in a 10–0 loss to Baltimore in the first game of a doubleheader. He goes 1-for-4 with a walk, two runs scored, and an RBI in the nightcap, won by the Red Sox 10–3.

September 23—Yaz goes 2-for-3 with a walk, scoring twice and putting the Red Sox ahead with a two-run homer in the fifth. But the Orioles rally to win 7–5.

September 24—Yaz goes 1-for-4 with a run scored and an RBI and is hit by a pitch as the Red Sox beat Baltimore 11–7.

September 26—Yaz goes 2-for-3 with a three-run homer off Luis Tiant, a double, and a walk and picks up an assist during a rundown play between third and home, but the Red Sox lose to Cleveland 6–3.

September 27—Yaz goes 1-for-3 with a walk in a 6–0 loss to Cleveland.

And his best was yet to come. In the last two games of the season, Yaz was going to be virtually invincible.

SATURDAY, SEPTEMBER 30

While we stumbled at home earlier in the week, losing twice to Cleveland, we had been extremely fortunate to get unexpected help from the California Angels, Kansas City Athletics, and Washington Senators. We didn't have to watch the scoreboard

Jose Santiago beat our long-time nemesis, the Minnesota Twins, on Saturday to set up the showdown for the pennant the next day. (*Courtesy of the Boston Red Sox*)

anymore. Nobody else could help us now. The youngest team in the league, the 100–1 shot, was going to have to do it all itself. If we didn't beat the Twins twice, "The Impossible Dream" was prematurely over.

On paper our task seemed impossible. The Twins had dominated us ever since I joined the Red Sox and had beaten us 11 times in 16 tries during the 1967 season. Minnesota was sending its two hottest starters to the mound against us. Jim Kaat's record was only 16–13, but he had gone 7–0 with a 1.56 ERA in September and completed six of his seven starts. With his sinker and his control, "Kitty" was the rare lefthander who was perfectly suited to pitching in Fenway Park. Dean Chance, who had won the Cy Young Award with the Angels three years earlier, was 20–13 with a no-hitter and an abbreviated perfect game to his credit and would be pitching Sunday's game. Chance was already 4–1 against us with a 1.58 ERA and two shutouts, including that perfect game. Furthermore, the Twins were a battle-hardened team. They had won the pennant two years before and knew what it took to win it again. Only a handful of us, and not one of our key players, had ever been in a pennant race for anywhere near this long.

Dick Williams pondered sending Lonborg back to the mound on two days' rest on Saturday. I don't know what changed his mind. Maybe it was because Kaat had beaten Lonnie 2–1 back in June, or maybe it was because if we didn't win on Sunday it wouldn't matter what happened on Saturday, and he wanted to have his ace going head-to-head with Minnesota's. Whatever Williams' reasons, Lonnie got a sorely needed extra day of rest. Jose Santiago, who had made four relief appearances against the Twins during the season with mixed results, would oppose Kaat. Santiago was 11–4 but had made only 10 starts, although in his last four spot starts he had pitched very well, allowing just 23 hits in 34 ⅔ innings while posting a 1.82 ERA.

"He was the best we had at that time," said Williams.

Red Sox fans were praying Santiago wouldn't be another Denny Galehouse, the surprise Red Sox starter who got thumped by Cleveland in the one-game playoff for the pennant in 1948. Nineteen years later Galehouse's name was still mud in Boston.

But the 27-year-old Santiago, who was about to go out and pitch the most important game of his life, was confident and, perhaps more importantly, loose in the clubhouse before the game.

We all were. Music was playing, and guys were joking around. Santiago, who did some broadcasting of winter league baseball games back home in Puerto Rico, walked around from locker to locker with a tape recorder doing mock interviews with us in different voices, including Count Dracula's. Jose was a good mimic, and he cracked us up. Then he turned serious, sidled up to Yaz, and told him: "I promise you that Killebrew isn't going to hit any out of the park off me today, okay?"

Yaz and Harmon Killebrew were tied for the league lead in homers with 43 apiece, and I couldn't help but think back to 1963 when Dick Stuart had been dueling Killebrew for the home run crown and watched Red Sox pitchers comically serve up five homers to him in the series. There was much, much more than a home run title at stake now.

"Jose, you make sure none of his go out," Yaz promised, shaking Santiago's hand, "and I'll make sure I hit one out for you."

Fenway Park was rocking with 32,909 rabid fans packed into the stands when Santiago took the mound. Mel Parnell, our TV color analyst who always believed he should have been the one to start that playoff game against the Indians, had said that Galehouse turned ghostly white when he found the game ball in his shoe that morning in 1948. Santiago didn't blanch when bullpen coach Al Lakeman, as was his custom, handed him the game ball and asked for it back after nine innings. But his nerves got him when he started delivering his warm-up pitches. "Who would not feel nervous in a game like that?" he admitted later.

Zoilo Versalles, the league's MVP in 1965, led off the game with a single, and Killebrew drew a one-out walk. Two-time batting king Tony Oliva lined a single to right, and the Twins quickly led 1–0. A single by Bob Allison loaded the bases, and the fans were wondering if this was going to be a reprise of 1948. Rod Carew, destined to be the AL Rookie of the Year in 1967, lined a Santiago pitch the other way but right into the glove of Jerry Adair at third base, and we all breathed a sigh of relief. Jose fell behind Ted Uhlaender 3-and-1 but got him to ground the next pitch to Mike Andrews at second and end the inning.

"In the first inning I was wild high. I wasn't bending my back, and I was pitching too quick," Santiago said. "In the second inning I got in the groove and had great stuff."

Meanwhile "Kitty" Kaat was just as sharp as he had been all month. We did touch him for three singles, but he struck out four of the first nine batters he faced. While striking out Santiago, however, he grabbed his left elbow and yelped in severe pain. He had pulled a tendon in the joint. Kaat tried to pitch through it, but after lobbing two weak balls to Andrews he had to leave the game. Jim Perry relieved him. We had caught another major break.

The Twins threatened again in the fourth after Ken Harrelson got twisted up trying to catch Uhlaender's fly in right field and had it bounce off his glove for a one-out triple. Santiago came back from a 3-and-0 count to fan Jerry Zimmerman and then retired Perry on a fly ball.

We finally broke through in the fifth and brought the crowd to life. Reggie Smith led off with a double, and Williams sent up Dalton Jones to pinch hit for catcher Russ Gibson. Jones hit what appeared to be a routine grounder to second, but the ball took a bad hop, struck Carew in the shoulder, and turned into an infield hit, putting runners at first and third. The rally started to wither when Perry fanned both Santiago and Andrews, but Adair dumped a single into right-center to tie the game and send Jones to third. Now Yaz was at the plate, and he pulled a pitch into the hole that both Carew and Killebrew, who was playing first, went after. Carew gloved it in plenty of time to throw Yaz out, but Perry neglected to cover the base, and Yaz streaked across the bag with a gift hit as Jones scored to put us ahead 2–1. It's unimaginable that Kaat, who won 14 Gold Gloves during his career, would have made such a boneheaded mistake. Another break.

Minnesota tied it in the sixth after Santiago walked Allison and gave up singles to Uhlaender and pinch hitter Rich Reese. But the Twins wasted a terrific opportunity to break the game open by leaving the bases loaded.

Ron Kline, who hadn't lost a game all year (7–0) and was usually tough on us, started the bottom of the sixth for Minnesota, and George Scott greeted him by depositing his first pitch into the center-field bleachers for a home run. We were so excited we nearly tore Boomer's uniform off when he got back to the dugout!

It was still 3–2 an inning later when Andrews beat out a topped ball in front of the plate. Adair hit a comebacker to Kline that should have been an inning-ending double play, but Versalles dropped the throw for an error. Yet another break! With Yaz due up, Minnesota manager Cal Ermer went to the bullpen again, this time for lefty Jim Merritt. Merritt worked Yaz carefully, as all the league's pitchers had learned to do in 1967, fell behind on the count 3-and-1, and had to groove a fastball. Yaz blasted it into the Minnesota bullpen for his 44th homer of the season, a three-run shot that gave us a 6–2 advantage. Fenway Park erupted like a volcano.

Gary Bell took over for a tiring Santiago in the eighth. A few days earlier Bell had made a light-hearted but interesting observation. He had won 12 games for us since being traded from Cleveland in June but had also lost two games to us while pitching for the Indians. So he had actually been responsible for 14 of our victories. "Never has a man on two teams done so much toward winning a pennant," he cracked. "If we win the pennant by two games, the games I lost to the Red Sox will be the difference."

If we were going to win the pennant now, it would be by the thin margin of one game, and Bell's two losses to the Red Sox were going to make all the difference. But right now he had a four-run lead to protect if his contributions were going to matter at all. He did until two were out in the ninth when Cesar Tovar doubled and Killebrew hit one over the screen, cutting our lead to two. (I guess Bell hadn't promised Yaz, who finished the day 3-for-4 with four RBIs, that Killebrew wouldn't connect against him.) Bell shook it off, retired Oliva on a liner to third, and we won 6–4, pulling into a tie with the Twins for first place. The Tigers could have made it a three-way deadlock. But after winning the first game of their doubleheader with California 5–0, they had blown a 6–2 lead in the eighth inning of the nightcap and lost 8–6.

All we had accomplished was keeping our chances alive for one more day, but it was impossible not to celebrate in the clubhouse like we'd already won the pennant. The only thing missing was the champagne. Jim Lonborg, however, remained subdued. He stayed in the trainer's room, mentally preparing himself for the biggest game of his life against a team he had never beaten in six career decisions. The Twins had accounted for one-third of his nine losses in 1967.

Brilliant people like Lonborg aren't usually superstitious. But he had acquired some superstitions in 1967, like going to the movies on Friday afternoons before pitching a home game that night. He'd also been more successful on the road than at home in 1967, posting a 13–4 record with a 2.22 ERA compared to his 8–5 record and 4.66 ERA at Fenway. So that night Lonnie didn't go home. Instead he bunked with Hawk Harrelson in his room at the Sheraton-Boston Hotel.

"I thought if I slept in a hotel, it might make me feel like I was pitching a road game," he explained.

SUNDAY, OCTOBER 1

One hundred and sixty-one games had brought us to the brink of the Red Sox' first pennant in 21 years. Not since 1949 had the Red Sox even come this close. It was all coming down to this one game against the team that for years had tormented us more than any other. Back in April the odds-makers in Las Vegas had made us 100–1 shots to win the pennant. I'm sure the odds on us were much better today than they had been six months earlier, but I'm equally sure they were still considerably less than even.

Shortly before the game Dick Williams called a team meeting. This was unusual because Dick didn't call many meetings. About the only time he would ever address us as a team was on the bus after we'd lost a tough game. "Boys, just letting you know you'd better be in your rooms tonight," he'd say. And he bed-checked us a lot. But he wasn't going to chastise us this time. It wasn't a rah-rah pep talk, and it wasn't very long. It couldn't wait until after the game because, win or lose, the clubhouse was going to be packed with writers, some of whom had flown in from other cities to cover this improbable series, and well-wishers if we won or mourners if we lost.

"I want to congratulate you men right now on a great season," he said solemnly. "I want to thank you all for all you have given me. I know that you feel you can beat Minnesota today, and so do I. So let's go get 'em."

It's hard to imagine that Fenway Park could have been rocking any more than it had been the previous afternoon. But it was. An overflow crowd of 35,770 had squeezed inside to witness the final showdown, and hundreds of thousands more who couldn't get tickets were watching the game on television. Today, unlike the day before, we were all nervous. The Twins had given away Saturday's game by making mistakes like Zoilo Versalles' error and Jim Perry's brain lock. Today we were making the mistakes.

As an extra incentive Lonborg had inked "$10,000," the possible amount of a winning World Series share, in the pocket of his glove. He retired the first two batters but got too careful with Harmon Killebrew and walked him on four pitches. Tony Oliva lashed a double to left that Yaz retrieved quickly enough to have forced Killebrew to stop at third. But third base coach Billy Martin waved him home. He should have been an easy out, especially with two players destined to win Gold Gloves that year handling the ball. George Scott cut off Yaz's throw in the middle of the diamond, but his relay to Russ Gibson was high and off the mark as Killebrew slid under the catcher with the first run of the game.

The Twins made it 2–0 in the third inning, courtesy of a rare error by Yastrzemski. Again Lonborg issued a two-out walk, this time to speedy Cesar Tovar. Killebrew lined a single to left-center that Yaz charged . . . and overran. The ball kept rolling all the way to The Wall as Tovar raced home from first.

We should have been discouraged. If our two best defensive players were messing up like this, what chance did the rest of us have? But we weren't discouraged. Before the game we had talked among ourselves and agreed that in order to beat the Twins we had to be aggressive. We couldn't play it safe and wait for something good to happen. We had to make it happen. At least the mistakes we were making were errors of aggression, not errors of timidity.

If we were discouraged at all, it was by our bad luck against Dean Chance. Lonborg led off the bottom of the third with a single but was rubbed out when Jerry Adair grounded into a double play. Yaz, whom Minnesota pitchers could not get out this day, opened the fourth with a double. Hawk Harrelson flied to right, and then Boomer hit a screaming line drive that was ticketed for center field. But Chance speared it and threw to second to double up Yaz and end the threat.

The score was still 2–0 when we batted in the bottom of the sixth, and the crowd was getting restless. Chance had allowed only four hits, and only one runner had gotten as far as second base. Those two runs were beginning to look like 20. Lonborg was scheduled to lead off the inning, and most everyone inside Fenway Park and watching on TV expected Williams would send up a pinch hitter. Lonborg, after all, had come into the game batting .126. But what the fans didn't realize was that Lonnie had been swinging a much better bat in September and was hitting a respectable .235 over his last eight games with a double, triple, and three RBIs. Most of his hits down the stretch had been important ones. Down by a run in the sixth inning against Washington on August 21, Lonnie had triggered a three-run rally with a single in a game we eventually won 6–5. He had an RBI single in a 2–1 victory over the Yankees eight days later and an RBI double in a 3–1 triumph over New York on September 7. Five days after that he tripled home the winning run in the eighth inning of a 3–1 victory over Kansas City.

Lonnie already had one of our four hits off Chance in this one. So Williams let him bat. I wasn't surprised, and neither was anybody else in the dugout. He was our ace, and we had to keep him in the game. We still had 12 outs left. But I never expected Lonnie to bunt.

Lonnie checked the defensive alignment before stepping into the batter's box and noticed that third baseman Cesar Tovar was not on the edge of the grass looking for a bunt.

"My first time up Chance threw me a fastball right down the middle, and I slapped it for a single. From that I felt he wasn't going to waste any pitches on me," Lonborg explained later. He guessed Chance would not nibble but would challenge him with fastballs. "A fastball in the middle of the plate is the best pitch to bunt. I can run better than most guys on the team, and I knew I could get the hit if I got the ball on the ground."

He did. It was a perfectly placed bunt down the third base line, and Tovar had to eat the ball. Lonnie was aboard with a leadoff single, and the worried crowd at last began to stir. A veteran team like the Twins would have clapped their hands a little and calmly said: "Okay, here it comes." A rally would have been expected by a team like that. But we didn't have that kind of swagger. We were jumping up and down in the dugout like Little Leaguers. Nobody in that crowd was more excited than we were. You might ask how a little bunt can change the course of a game. Well, anything can, I guess, just like Dave Roberts' stolen base did for the Red Sox 37 years later against the Yankees in the 2004 American League Championship Series. You just don't imagine a bunt could have that much of an impact in a game of this magnitude. Obviously the Twins didn't, or they would have been guarding against it. But it did. When Lonnie got that bunt down, it gave us an incredible lift, and bang, bang, bang, things began to happen.

Adair grounded a ball up the middle and into center field for a single, and the tying runs were on base. Dalton Jones got the sign to sacrifice both runners into scoring position. But after fouling off a pitch as Minnesota's corner infielders charged hard, Williams took off the bunt and let Jones swing away. Dalton slapped the ball past the charging Tovar for another single, and the bases were loaded with nobody out and Yaz coming up. Could anything have been more perfect?

Fenway Park was absolute bedlam now. It was a Wall of Sound legendary record producer Phil Spector would have envied. For the first time in a month, Yaz wasn't thinking about hitting a home run.

"I just wanted to hit the ball hard somewhere and get some runs in," Yaz said. "He gave me a pitch that I could have hit out of the park, but I hit it for a single."

Center fielder Ted Uhlaender charged the ball as it skipped over second base, but he couldn't prevent Lonnie and Adair from scoring and Jones from racing around to third. The game was tied 2–2.

With no outs and the go-ahead run on third, Minnesota manager Cal Ermer brought the infield in to cut off the run. Ken Harrelson worked the count full, then hit a high chopper to Versalles at shortstop. It was a contact play, and Dalton was off as soon as Hawk's bat met the ball. Because Versalles had to wait for the ball to come down, he had no chance to get Jones at the plate. But he threw it there anyway, and Dalton easily beat it. We were ahead for the first time, 3–2, and now the Twins were making the critical mistakes again.

Ermer had seen enough from Chance and went to the bullpen for Al Worthington. Worthington was a 12-year veteran who had pitched in the 1965 World Series. But he threw like a raw rookie against us that day. With George Scott at the plate, he tossed two wild pitches to let Yaz score and move pinch runner Jose Tartabull around to third. Boomer fanned for the first out of the inning, but Worthington walked me. Reggie Smith hit a sharp grounder down to Killebrew at first base, and he played it like Tony Horton. The ball struck him in the knee, and Tartabull scored on the error. Worthington finally got the last two outs, but we led 5–2 and still had our ace in the game.

Lonborg breezed through the seventh but ran into some trouble in the eighth. Rich Reese pinch hit for Versalles and led off the inning with a single. Tovar chopped a ball toward second that Adair fielded in the base path. With Tovar's speed Adair knew he didn't have time to start a conventional double play by pitching the ball to me covering second. He tagged Reese and tossed the ball to first in time to get Tovar. But Reese had spiked him in the left leg while trying to avoid the tag and opened up a nasty gash that would require seven stitches to close. Adair had to leave the game for treatment, and Mike Andrews took over at second.

Lonborg wasn't out of trouble yet. Killebrew and Oliva stroked two-out singles, and Bob Allison lined another hit down the left-field line toward the corner. Killebrew scored, but Allison, representing the tying run and eager to get into scoring position, tried to stretch the hit into a double even though Yaz had hustled to cut off the ball. Yaz gunned him down with a perfect throw, his 17th assist of the season, and the rally was over.

"I thought I had two," Allison said afterward. "I looked at Carl and saw the throw coming, and I had to try and make it. But I didn't. It was just another great play by Yastrzemski."

Uhlaender led off the ninth with a groundball right to me. But the ball took a bad hop, just like Dalton Jones' ball to Carew the day before during our game-tying rally, and hit me in the Adam's apple. It stunned me, and I fell to my knees. Williams and Buddy LeRoux both ran out to see if I was okay.

"How are you? You wanna come out?" Dick asked.

"Are you kidding?" I croaked. "No way you're getting me out of here."

Dick laughed and went back to the dugout with Buddy.

But as I waited for the game to resume, the 1960 World Series and shortstop Tony Kubek popped into my mind. The Yankees were leading the Pirates 7–4 in the bottom of the eighth of Game 7 when Pittsburgh's Bill Virdon hit a double-play ball that took a bad hop on Kubek and struck him in the throat. The Pirates went on to score five runs in the inning and won the game 10–9 to capture the World Series. Could history be repeating itself right now?

It didn't. Lonnie got the fleet Carew to bang into a double play with Boomer making a nice scoop of Andrews' throw after Uhlaender tried to take him out of the play. The Twins were down to their last out. Ermer sent up Rich Rollins to bat for catcher Russ Nixon. Rollins was a right-handed hitter, and Lonborg had a good sinker. I yelled over to Dalton Jones at third: "Roomie, be ready! I think this ball may be coming our way!" Lonnie got a pitch in on Rollins' hands, and he popped it up in my direction, though not very high. I backpedaled onto the outfield grass, waited for the ball to come down, and caught it. It was a play I had been conditioned to make hundreds of times before, so it didn't hit me right away exactly what we had done. Not until Dalton started screaming. "Roomie! Roomie! We did it! We did it!" Then I said: "Holy Jeez! Wow!" And I started jumping up and down. I'd never been so excited in my life!

By now the fans were pouring out of the stands and onto the field to mob us. A year ago if they had come out of the stands,

That's me starting to celebrate after catching Rich Rollins' pop-up for the final out that clinched the pennant for us, the first by a Red Sox team in 21 years. (*Courtesy of the Boston Red Sox*)

they would have been swinging axes because we'd blown another game. Now they just wanted to slap us on the back and shake our hands. I tried to squirm my way through the crowd to give Lonnie the ball, but he'd been carried out toward right field on the shoulders of the fans. If we stayed out there we might get crushed, so one by one we wended our way into the dugout and through the tunnel to the clubhouse. It was there I finally gave the ball to Lonnie, who was one of the last to make it off the field.

"I was lucky to get out of there alive!" he exclaimed. "They tore off my T-shirt, my sweatshirt, and even part of my shoes!"

General manager Dick O'Connell (left) gave Yaz a congratulatory handshake in the clubhouse—and a $100,000 contract for 1968—after we clinched the pennant and fulfilled "The Impossible Dream." (*Courtesy of the Boston Red Sox*)

So far we hadn't won anything. All we had done by sweeping the Twins was assure ourselves of a three-game playoff series against Detroit if the Tigers swept their doubleheader with the Angels. We knew the Tigers had already won the first game 6–4. We celebrated like college frat boys in the clubhouse, swilling beer, smoking cigars, and squirting each other with shaving cream, but keeping the champagne on ice. Mr. Yawkey came down from his private roof box to congratulate us, and there were tears in his eyes. Dick O'Connell was there, too, and he asked Yaz if he thought a raise to $100,000 in 1968 was fair. Yaz, who had been earning $58,000, said it was.

The second game of the doubleheader in Detroit was beginning, and the radio signal was being piped to Boston. Buddy LeRoux had a radio in the trainer's room and tuned it to the game, but there was only enough room in there for about eight people. The events were relayed to everyone else in the clubhouse as they unfolded. The Tigers grabbed a 3–1 lead in the second inning, but a two-run homer by Don Mincher put the Angels ahead 4–3 in the third. Someone found another radio, plugged it into a wall in the clubhouse, and now we could all follow the progress of the game. We cheered every out like we were fans. Roger Repoz slammed a two-run triple in the fourth, and California's lead was up to 7–3. It was 8–5 when the Tigers came to bat in the bottom of the ninth. The first two batters reached, and then George Brunet got Jim Price to fly out. That brought up Dick McAuliffe, a second baseman with 22 homers who could tie up the game with one swing and who had grounded into just one double play all year. He swung but hit the ball on the ground sharply to second baseman Bobby Knoop, who flipped it to shortstop Jim Fregosi for the out at second. Fregosi's relay nailed McAuliffe, and we were the champions of the American League!

Now the celebration really began. Yaz, who had gone 7-for-8 with six RBIs in the two games against the Twins and wrapped up the Triple Crown with a .326 average, 44 homers, and 121 RBIs, came out of the chair in front of his locker like he was riding a Saturn rocket. "We won it! We played six weeks without one of the greatest players in the American League—Tony Conigliaro—and still wouldn't quit!"

Even Williams dropped his tough-guy posture and became emotional. "It's over! It's over! It's unbelievable!"

The champagne was uncorked and flowed freely. We all crowded around Yaz and thanked him for the great year he'd had to get us this far. Mr. Yawkey came down from his office to visit the clubhouse for the second time, and he was almost crying. He had given up drinking a few years before, but someone handed him a paper cup filled with champagne. He went up to Williams and said: "I want to have a toast with you, Dick."

Williams grabbed a glass of champagne and said: "Here's to you, sir, for giving me the opportunity."

But the gratitude was all Mr. Yawkey's. This was only the second pennant he had won in his 34 years owning the Red Sox. "And here's to you, Dick, for making the best of it. This is the happiest moment of my life."

Never had a team in the history of baseball done what we had done, go from ninth place to a pennant in one year. "The Impossible Dream" had become reality.

9

THE DAWN

"Everything the Red Sox are today, all the sellouts, stems from 1967. That team can never be honored enough. Nineteen Sixty-Seven is the great dividing line in Red Sox history."

—Boston Globe *columnist Bob Ryan*

Boston Baseball Writers Dinner

January 12, 2006

THE WORLD SERIES

The worst thing about a wonderful dream is that eventually you have to wake up. We woke up 10 days too soon in 1967.

Our opponents in the World Series were the St. Louis Cardinals, a talented and veteran club. They had won the World Series three years earlier, beating the New York Yankees in seven games, and every one of their regulars had Series experience. Not one of ours had ever played in one. The odds-makers made us 3–1 underdogs, which didn't sound encouraging until you remembered the 100–1 odds against us at the start of the season.

The Cardinals were also well rested. They had clinched the National League pennant back on September 18, and it had been conceded to them weeks before that. They won 101 games and outdistanced the second-place San Francisco Giants by 10½ games. Even fresher was their ace, Bob Gibson. A line drive off the bat of Pittsburgh's Roberto Clemente had fractured his leg back on July 15, and Gibson hadn't begun pitching again until early September. "I think the rest helped," he said before the World Series began. Gibson had been a 20-game winner for the Cardinals in 1965 and 1966, and he had blinded the Yankees in

The two managers, Dick Williams (left) and Red Schoendienst, exchange handshakes and smiles before the first game of the World Series. By the third game, they were accusing each other of ordering their pitchers to throw at hitters. (*Courtesy of the Boston Red Sox*)

the 1964 Series, winning two games and setting a record with 31 strikeouts. He threw hard, and he was nasty.

We read some stuff in the papers where the Cardinals said we didn't belong on the same field with them. We cut out the articles to use as incentive, but they didn't help us whenever we faced Gibson.

Our pitchers were drained from a 162-game race that came down to the final day, and they had only two days to recover before the first game of the Series on October 4 at Fenway Park. We had also lost the services of left-handed reliever Sparky Lyle, who had gone 1–2 with five saves, a 2.28 ERA, and 42 strikeouts in 43 ⅓ innings in 27 games since joining us at mid-season. Lyle had strained a ligament in his elbow late in the season. The Red Sox petitioned Commissioner William Eckert for special dispensation to make left-handed teen rookie Ken Brett eligible for the Series, and the request was granted. Brett, who had just turned 19, had gone 14–11 with a 1.95 ERA at Class A Winston-Salem and Class AA Pittsfield with 219 strikeouts in 189 innings but had pitched only two innings for us in September. "Kemer" would become the youngest pitcher to ever appear in a World Series, but due to his inexperience Dick Williams could not risk using him in a meaningful situation.

Needless to say, tickets were extremely scarce around Boston. Red Sox fans had been waiting for 21 years for the World Series to return to Fenway Park, and after the 1,800 season's ticket holders had been taken care of, there were 100 requests for every available ticket. To give as many fans as possible a shot at seeing a game, nobody could buy more than two tickets, and nobody could get tickets for all four games in Boston. Fans got tickets for Games 1 and 7 or Games 2 and 6.

GAME 1

Williams tapped Jose Santiago to pitch against Gibson in front of an SRO crowd of 34,796 at Fenway. Santiago gave it his best, but

Gibson was just too dominant. Gibson hurled a six-hitter and struck out 10, getting me three times. The Cardinals won the game 2–1.

Lou Brock, a future Hall of Famer, set the tone for the entire Series by leading off the game with a single and stealing second. His seven steals in the Series would be a record, and later on he would become the all-time steals king with 938 until Rickey Henderson broke his record two decades later. Brock scored the first St. Louis run in the third inning after singling again, taking third on a double by Curt Flood, and coming home on a groundout by Roger Maris. Santiago tied it up for us in the bottom of the inning by hitting a home run into the screen.

Carl Yastrzemski, the American League MVP and Triple Crown winner, had a great World Series for us, hitting .400 with three homers and striking out only once in 25 at-bats. (*Courtesy of the Boston Red Sox*)

Carl Yastrzemski kept the tie intact by throwing out Julian Javier trying to score from second on another Brock single in the fourth. But Brock, who was 4-for-4 with a walk, finally beat us in the seventh. He never should have scored, though, because I tagged him out earlier in the inning.

Brock led off the inning with a single and lit out for second. I was covering the bag, and Russ Gibson's throw came in a bit high. I gloved it and tagged Brock's hand about six inches in front of the base.

"No, no!" bellowed umpire Frank Umont, calling Brock safe.

"What?" I shrieked. Umont said Brock's hand had gotten in ahead of the tag, and that was that. I never argued much with umpires. It had been a bang-bang play, that was his call, and there was nothing more I could do. Brock moved over to third on a groundout by Flood, and Maris brought him home for the second time with another groundball. Gibson, also destined for the Hall of Fame, made the slender lead stand up.

GAME 2

Whereas Brock had set the tone for the Cardinals the previous afternoon, Jim Lonborg set the tone for us immediately this time. "Gentleman" Jim's first pitch of the game buzzed Brock under the chin and sent him sprawling, much to the delight of the 35,188 fans crammed inside Fenway.

"You bush so-and-so!" someone yelled from the Cardinals dugout.

"I just looked over there out of the corner of my eye and had to laugh," Lonnie said. "What do they think I'm going to do? Give them home plate?"

Lonnie had the Cardinals intimidated for the remainder of the game. He faced some great hitters and made them look silly. The only guy who seemed to have a clue was their second baseman, Julian Javier. Dick Hughes, a rookie, shut us out for three innings, but in the fourth Yaz socked a homer to put us in front 1–0. We picked up another run in the seventh after loading the bases on walks to George Scott and Reggie Smith and an error by third baseman Mike Shannon. Ron Willis relieved Hughes, and I brought Boomer home with a sacrifice fly. Yaz hit his second homer of the game, a three-run shot off lefty Joe Hoerner in the eighth, and we led 5–0.

Lonborg, meanwhile, was working on a perfect game until Flood took a close 3-and-2 pitch and drew a walk with one out in the seventh. We made a couple of good plays behind him to keep the no-hitter going. Second baseman Jerry Adair, playing with seven stitches in his leg after getting spiked in the Minnesota series, ranged up the middle to grab a ball off the bat of Brock and threw him out in the fourth. The walk to Flood turned out to be a momentary blessing. With two outs Orlando Cepeda hit a shot up the middle, this time to my side of second base. The ball was already past me when I extended my left arm, reached back, and snared it. There was no way I could have thrown out Cepeda at first. But I did have time to flip the ball to Adair covering second and force Flood.

A blister had developed on Lonborg's thumb in the sixth inning, however, and he had to limit the number of curveballs he was throwing if he wanted to remain in the game. Now relying primarily on his fastball, he was four outs away from the second no-hitter in World Series history when he threw a curve to Javier and hung it. Javier, who'd been right on Lonnie's pitches all afternoon, yanked it into the left-field corner for a double with two outs in the eighth.

"I just didn't make a good pitch to Javier. I might have if I wasn't having trouble with my thumb," Lonborg lamented. "I tried to reach back and give him my good breaking ball. But it wouldn't do what I wanted it to. It just hung there, and he hit it.

I just put my left hand over my eyes like a person would when he just saw a bad car wreck."

Lonborg got the last four outs and finished with the fourth one-hitter in Series history. And he left the Cardinals steaming. In addition to brushing back Brock, he'd also buzzed Dal Maxvill.

"We let him get away with it this time," Flood seethed. "But we can play that game, too. And we won't get Petrocelli or someone like that. We're gonna get Yastrzemski."

GAME 3

And they did when the World Series moved to St. Louis on October 7. When Yaz came to bat in the first inning, Nelson Briles hit him in the back of the leg with a pitch. Dick Williams bolted from the dugout and confronted plate umpire Frank Umont. "Are we going to have a throwing contest?" he demanded.

Umont summoned Cardinals manager Red Schoendienst from the St. Louis dugout, and he insisted Briles had not thrown at Yaz intentionally. But he argued: "We hear so much about Lonborg brushing guys back."

"Yeah," Williams agreed. "But there's a difference between brushing someone back and intentionally hitting him."

Umont chose not to issue any warnings, and the game resumed. But Jose Santiago, who was scheduled to pitch the next day, was fuming.

"If those bush-leaguers want to play baseball that way, that's all right with me," he said. "Maybe we'll find out how they like it when a couple of their boys get drilled."

Meanwhile Gary Bell just didn't have it. Lou Brock led off the bottom of the first with a triple and scored on a single by Curt Flood, and Mike Shannon socked a two-run homer in the second to put St. Louis ahead 3–0. After George Thomas pinch hit for Bell in the third, Gary Waslewski took over on the mound and tossed three perfect innings with three strikeouts, earning a start in Game 6 . . . if we got to a Game 6. We lost the game 5–2.

GAME 4

Santiago wasn't around long enough to drill anyone. The Cardinals combed him for six hits and four runs in just two-thirds of an inning. That was more than enough for Bob Gibson, who tamed us with a five-hitter and shut us out 6–0 to give St. Louis a commanding 3–1 edge in the Series. Gibson only fanned six this time, but he was no less overpowering. After George Scott took three called strikes in his first at-bat, he commented: "I didn't see one of them. I had to turn around and ask (catcher Tim) McCarver where the ball went. He told me right over the outside corner. I told him: 'That's what I thought, but I couldn't see it.'"

Boomer did get one of our five hits off Gibson.

GAME 5

Now we were 27 outs away from elimination, and it was up to our ace, Jim Lonborg, to beat St. Louis and send the World Series back to Boston, where we had compiled a 49–32 record during the regular season. The Cardinals were confident Lonnie would not master them the way he did at Fenway, not at Busch Stadium.

"In a park with a good background to hit like ours, he won't be that tough," Curt Flood predicted.

But he was. Lonnie did give up three hits instead of one, but he was one out away from another shutout when Roger Maris spoiled it with a home run. When Lonnie came to bat in the seventh inning, Tim McCarver, squatting down behind the plate, quipped: "Well, we're really hitting you again today. We got two biggies off you." The two "biggies" were a one-out single by Dal Maxvill in the third and a one-out single by Maris in the fourth.

We won 3–1, but we didn't give Lonborg much room for error. Steve Carlton, yet another future Hall of Famer on the Cardinals' roster, was equally tough for the Cardinals.

We nicked Carlton for an unearned run in the third inning. Joe Foy singled with one out, and Mike Andrews reached when third baseman Mike Shannon messed up his bunt. Carlton struck out Yaz, but Ken Harrelson delivered a single to plate Foy.

That was the only run we got until the ninth when we picked up a couple more runs off Ron Willis and Jack Lamabe, a former teammate of ours from the Country Club days. George Scott drew a walk to start the inning, and Reggie Smith doubled. After Willis walked me intentionally, Red Schoendienst went to the bullpen for Lamabe. Elston Howard greeted him with a single, and when Maris mishandled the ball in right field, Smith came around to score and make it 3–0. Williams signaled for a double steal with two outs, but the Cardinals were ready for it, and I got trapped in a rundown between third and home. Still, we had enough for Lonnie, who wasn't hurt by Maris' two-out homer in the bottom of the ninth.

Oh, I should mention that Eddie Bressoud, the guy I had replaced two years earlier, finished the game at shortstop for the Cardinals. He'd been unhappy when he'd lost the shortstop's job to me, and he was just a backup infielder now, but he was going to get a World Series championship ring to cherish for the rest of his life.

An enthusiastic crowd of about 1,500 fans greeted us at Logan Airport when we returned to Boston. That was only about 10 percent the size of the crowd that had overwhelmed us when we had returned from that trip in July with a 10-game winning streak, but it was comforting to know they were still behind us.

GAME 6

We unloaded on the Cardinals in front of another SRO crowd of 35,188 at Fenway Park, blasting four homers. I hadn't done much with the bat in the first five games, getting just one hit and one RBI in 14 at-bats. But I got us cranked up with a homer off Dick Hughes in the second inning. Lou Brock, however, put the Cardinals in front 2–1 in the third, singling home the tying run, stealing second, and scoring on a single by Flood.

That was the only damage they could to do Gary Waslewski, however. We did a lot of damage to Hughes in the bottom of the fourth. Yaz started things with a homer, his third of the World Series, and then Reggie Smith and I went deep back to back to make the score 4–2. It was the first time in World Series history a team had hit three homers in an inning. That was a thrill.

Waslewski tired in the sixth and turned the game over to John Wyatt. And in the seventh Brock did it to us again. Bobby Tolan, pinch hitting for Nelson Briles, walked, bringing Brock to the plate. We all knew Wyatt would try to get Brock out with a spitter. He turned around and said to me: "I'm gonna get The Big One." That was the blob of Vaseline he hid under his belt. Well, he loaded up the ball and threw it to Brock, who swung and hit it so hard it sounded like a cannon going off. Brock was always good for a few homers every year, and he'd hit a career-best 21 of them in 1967. But I never expected to see him hit a ball like that! Now that I think of it, we probably should have checked his bat for cork. Anyway, it seemed like it took five minutes for it to come down. The ball soared way over the 420 mark in center field and beyond the exit in the bleachers. As Brock trotted around the bases, having just tied up the game at 4–4, I strolled over to the mound to talk to Wyatt.

"I thought you were going to get The Blob, The Big One," I said.

"I did!" Wyatt exclaimed. "He must have hit the dry side!"

Boy, did he ever! I had to fight myself to keep from laughing as I went back to shortstop.

We came right back with a game-winning four-run rally in the bottom of the seventh. Dalton Jones stroked a one-out single off Jack Lamabe, and Joe Foy doubled him home to put us back on top 5–4. Joe Hoerner relieved Lamabe and gave up singles to Mike Andrews and Yaz that produced another run. Larry Jaster became the third pitcher of the inning for St. Louis, and Jerry Adair pinch hit for Jose Tartabull and hit a sacrifice fly that scored Andrews. Boomer and Smith followed with singles, scoring Yaz, and it was 8–4 as the crowd celebrated wildly. Ray Washburn relieved Jaster and, wary of me because of my two homers, walked me intentionally to load the bases before Elston Howard grounded out to end the inning.

That was the final score, and we had rallied from two games down to send the World Series to a decisive seventh game. The Cardinals would have their ace, Bob Gibson, on the mound, and we would counter with ours, Jim Lonborg, although he'd be pitching on just two days' rest.

The weather forecast called for showers overnight, and the grounds crew spread the tarp over the infield. Several years later general manager Dick O'Connell revealed that he had been sorely tempted to leave the field uncovered and turn on the sprinklers during the night so that the grounds would be unplayable the next day. A postponement would give Lonnie a badly needed extra day of rest. "Damn! I wished I'd had the guts to do it!" O'Connell said ruefully.

GAME 7

A worn-out Lonborg got through the first two innings and almost made it through the third unscathed. Light-hitting Dal Maxvill led off the third with a triple, but Lonnie bore down and retired Gibson and Brock. Then he ran out of steam. Curt Flood singled to center, scoring Maxvill with the first run of the game, and Roger Maris followed with another single, sending Flood around to third. Lonnie tossed a wild pitch, and Flood dashed home to make it 2–0.

The Cardinals doubled their lead in the fifth. Gibson homered, and Brock singled and stole second and third. Maris brought him in with a sacrifice fly. By now the sellout crowd of 35,188 was subdued. We were down 4–0 against Gibson and didn't even have a hit yet.

George Scott remedied that in the bottom of the fifth by leading off with a triple and scoring when second baseman Julian Javier heaved the relay into the St. Louis dugout. But the Cardinals put the game out of reach in the sixth when Javier belted a three-run homer. Lonborg, who had given up just four hits and one run in the first two games of the World Series, was battered for 10 hits in six-plus innings by the Cardinals before Williams mercifully lifted him. Gibson threw his third complete game of the Series, a three-hitter, and struck out 10 more batters. We lost 7–2.

"Lonnie had a great year," Dick Williams recalled four decades later. "But Bob Gibson was the best right-hander I ever saw over a number of years."

Gibson and Brock were the difference in the World Series. Gibson was 3–0 with a 1.00 ERA and 26 strikeouts in 27 innings, and Brock hit .414 with 12 hits, including two doubles, a triple, and a homer, eight runs scored, and seven stolen bases. Yaz had a superb Series himself, hitting .400 with two doubles, three homers, five RBIs, and four walks, and he struck out just once in 25 at-bats. Forty years later Williams was still proclaiming that Yaz had the greatest year he'd ever seen a ballplayer have. "In my 50-odd years in baseball," he said, "I never saw another player have the kind of year Yaz had for me. Running, throwing, hitting, hitting with power . . . he did it all." But Yaz alone couldn't carry us to the World Series championship that had eluded the Red Sox since 1918 and would continue to elude them for another 36 years.

It was a tremendous disappointment not to win the World Series after all we had accomplished in 1967 when absolutely nothing had been expected of us. But the front page of the *Boston Record-American* the next morning summed up the season best. It was a valentine that read: "They Lost the Series but Won Our Hearts."

Impossible Dream: Looking Back More than Half a Century Later

There are ups and down in any sport, periods of feast and famine. But in the 120 years of Red Sox baseball, one can clearly see 1967 as a dividing line, and so much that is so good has followed that defining year.

What became most palpably different is found in the experience of the fans of the Red Sox. There was a sea change in 1967, and things have never been the same since. That's not to say there haven't been years that tested fan loyalties. Even in the last decade, we've seen the collapse of the season in 2011—first place on September 1, but nowhere by the end of the month. Then last place pretty much all year in 2012.

What followed that, but a World Series win in 2013? It was a special season pretty much from start to finish with a good number of players who held the hearts of fans. That the 2013 world championship followed the Boston Marathon bombing of that April only made the year that much more magical.

But immediately it was back to the depths, with last-place finishes again in both 2014 and 2015. Somehow it may be hard to remember but the team finished last three out of the four years from 2012 through 2015. A world championship to break up a stretch like that is always welcome.

The team had enjoyed a good period 100 years earlier. After winning the first World Series ever played, in 1903, and having the National League's New York Giants decline to play them in 1904, there followed a few rough years (1906 was abysmal, with a record of 49-105), but then they had a stretch embracing 1912, 1915, 1916, and 1918 in which they won four World Series. There's almost a parallel of sorts there to the 2004–2018 run. From 1918 on, though, until one got to 1946, things were *really* bad. From 1925 through 1932, they lost over 100 games in five of those eight years.

In 1946 they won the pennant, losing the World Series in seven games. They came within one win of the pennant in 1948 and 1949, but then they entered a doldrums again. Attendance at the park tended to hold over a million, until Ted Williams retired at the end of 1960. Then it plunged by a couple of hundred thousand fans a year. In 1965, only 652,201 came to the park. That's an average of 8,470 a game. The place was 75 percent empty. On September 16 of that year, this author saw Dave Morehead pitch a no-hitter against Cleveland. So did 1,246 other paying customers. That means the park had 32,277 empty seats.

Sure, there were fans. More came out for weekend games, or special occasions but Fenway Park felt dead a lot of the time. In 1967, that all changed. Suddenly, with an exciting, young, diverse team on the field, winning games and beginning to pursue a dream that had seemed impossible in April, attendance more than doubled what it had been the prior year, drawing 1,727,832—more than 100,000 more than had ever come to the park in any of the previous 66 seasons.

Never again did the Sox draw fewer than a million.

Red Sox fans have never been ones to follow the lure of bright, shiny objects. It never really mattered whether the seats were cramped, the ballpark old, the neighborhood something of a dull one. What mattered was the play on the field.

New Englanders value tradition, anyhow. We didn't need a spic and span but maybe soul-less ballpark. A retractable roof, climate-controlled conditions within? Ample parking right next door? Not necessary. Fair weather or foul, fans turn out at Fenway almost no matter what. Following the Red Sox is a part of the fabric of life in New England.

There were no renovations at Fenway Park, nothing really in the way of innovations or changes, until after new ownership arrived in the twenty-first century. Then came the Monster seats atop the left-field wall, and a number of improvements that cost in the tens of millions of dollars but set the park up to last for another 40 or 50 years. In 2012, the park celebrated its 100th anniversary.

The Seasons After '67

There were exciting seasons that followed 1967. There was 1972, when the Red Sox missed the pennant by a half-game. In 1975, they took the World Series to Game Seven. In 1978, they had a single-game playoff for the pennant. In 1986, they took the World Series to Game Seven. This was getting to be a "thing"—it was the fourth World Series in a row that had seen the Red Sox lose Game Seven. Cursed? They could never seem to win it all, but for the most part the fans stuck with them. Lovable losers? Maybe there was something there. Over the course of 12 seasons from 1998 through 1999, the Red Sox got into the playoffs five times—but could hardly even seem to win a game (they were swept in 1988, 1990, and 1995). They finally won a postseason game in 1998—but only one, losing three. They won another game in 1999, but lost four. They were 2–20 in postseason play from Game Six of the 1986 World Series to the end of the century.

It was remarkable, though. The passion for baseball—and Red Sox baseball in particular—never went away after 1967. Despite the discouraging ending to many seasons—even the ones when they did make it into the postseason—the fans kept the faith.

Some began to see a sort of virtue in this and began to worry whether the soul of the baseball fan in Boston would be sullied should the Red Sox ever win it all.

In the year of "Cowboy Up"—2003—it seemed possible we'd get to find out. Nope, the Red Sox did play deep into the postseason, but they lost to (who else?) the Yankees in Game Seven of that year's ALCS, and in extra innings, no less. In a game they seemed to have won. But no. Sales of *Curse of the Bambino* bumped up again.

The empirical method—put it to the test—that's what this author said. Yes, something of the Red Sox fan mystique might be lost if the Red Sox ever won a World Series. Heck, it had been 85 years. Let them win one and see what happens to the soul of the fans.

The 2003 season reignited a new era of good feelings in Red Sox Nation. New ownership had come aboard. Fenway Park was not going to be demolished and replaced by an imitation Fenway across the street. Nomar, David Ortiz, Manny, Johnny Damon, Kevin Millar, Tek, and Trot. Pedro still dominant. It was an exciting year, and from May 15 through the end of the season every single game was sold out.

That was true in 2004 as well—by the way, the Red Sox did finally win a World Series that year (more on that in a bit), and it was true in 2005. And 2006. And 2007, when the Sox won another World Series. And in 2008, 2009, 2010, 2011, and 2012. For 820 games in a row, the park was sold out.

After the last-place finish in 2012, hard on the heels of the disappointment that ended the 2011 season, there were some games that didn't sell out in 2013. But that year's team won yet another World Series. And in 2018, not only did they win the World Series for the fourth time in a 15-year stretch, but in getting to the Series the team won 108 regular-season games, setting a franchise record.

Let's reprise to 2004, just for a bit, and revel in the successes that see the Red Sox with more World Series wins than another team in the current century.

2004—Curve Reversed

First, a reminder of how the stage had been set. For those who lived through it, it was a time that will live in wonder for the rest of their lives. This author was one year old when the Red Sox lost Game Seven of the 1946 World Series. Nope, wasn't scarred by that one. But it was 21 years before the Sox got to playing in the postseason again. I saw them lose in Game Seven of the 1967 World Series, lose the pennant by a half-game in 1972, saw them lose Game Seven of the 1975 World Series, saw the 1978 single-game playoff loss, saw them lose Game Seven (and Game Six before it) of the 1986 World Series. After postseason play had expanded, saw them get swept in the ALCS in 1988 and get swept again in 1990. By that time, Sox fans were already primed for failure and everyone instinctively knew what Dan Shaughnessy's 1990 book *The Curse of the Bambino* was all about.

That sweep in 1990 was followed by the Red Sox being swept again in 1995, this time in the newly-created American League Division Series. They could top the division, but now it wasn't that they were reaching the final Game Sevens. They were swept and swept and swept. They lost 13 consecutive playoff games. In 1998, they won a game—beating the Indians in Game One of the Division Series. Hallelujah! But then lost the next three, and the ALDS. Who won the World Series that year? The New York Yankees. Of course. They swept the Padres.

In 1999, the Red Sox won the Division Series, and Yankees squared off against the Yankees in the best-of-seven League Championship Series. The Red Sox won one game (Pedro vs. Clemens), but only one. Who won the World Series that year? The New York Yankees. They swept the Braves.

In 2000, the Red Sox finished 2.5 games out of first place in the AL East—but who won the World Series that year? The New York Yankees. They nearly swept the Mets, losing just once. As of the final year of the 20th century, the Yankees held 26 world championships, starting with their first in 1923. During that stretch, the Ruth-less Boston Red Sox had won zero.

In 2003, the Red Sox reached the postseason again, via the Wild Card. The Yankees finished first. But the Sox edged Oakland, three games to two, and won the ALDS. And, head to head against the Yankees in the ALCS, they had shown up well. That series came down to a final Game Seven, and the Red Sox held a 5–2 lead, with only six outs to get. What could go wrong? Inevitably—so it felt to Sox fans inured to hopes being dashed—yes, it happened again. The Yankees won. The Red Sox lost.

So, come 2004, even after the Sox swept the Angels in the ALDS, no one really expected the Red Sox to beat the Yankees in a repeat performance of the ALCS. And after the team dropped the first two games in New York, needing to win four of the next five games in order to advance, fans could only hope against hope that they could somehow win Game Three, now that the games had come back to Fenway Park. Sorry, Red Sox fans. The Yankees slaughtered the Red Sox, 19–8. That would have been more discouraging if the Fenway faithful had truly believed there had been any chance. Maybe some of those born in 2000 harbored some hope—but not many who had truly been scarred by so many defeats over so many years. Losing 19–8 was like a final bucket of ice water thrown in the face of any who dared hope. Only an idiot would think the Red Sox had any chance; maybe win one game, sure. But no team had even come back from a three-to-one deficit in a postseason series and actually won. Tickets outside Fenway for Game Four were going for face value.

There were 25 idiots who dared hope—the 2004 Red Sox. Not only did they hope, but they pulled it off. They won Game Four in extra innings (thanks, Dave Roberts and thanks, David Ortiz.) They won Game Five in extra innings (thanks, David Ortiz.) And they kept rolling, winning Game Six in Yankee Stadium and then Game Seven in Yankee Stadium. And went on to sweep the St. Louis Cardinals in the 2004 World Series. We needn't go through the full story here. It's been told in multiple books, and earlier in this one, too.

The next day, and for several days thereafter, Red Sox fans woke up after a night's sleep and wondered if it had all been a dream. Had that *really* happened?

Yes, it had.

2007—Professionals at Play

The 2007 season is sometimes overlooked. It wasn't a miraculous season like 2004, it wasn't the team of bearded wonders that took up the "Boston Strong" motto in the wake of the bombing of the Boston Marathon that more or less opened the 2013 season. The 2007 Red Sox were a team of professionals, a team of excellent ballplayers who almost seemed to dominate all season long, and then sweep the Colorado Rockies in the 2007 World Series. It wasn't really as easy as it might seem in retrospect.

Yes, they were in first place in the AL East from April 18 all the way to the end of the season—150 consecutive game days in first place. But though they'd held leads of 10 or more games in midseason for considerable periods of time, they'd had to work their way there and then had to hold on. They finished with a record of 96-66, but were only two games ahead of the New York Yankees in the AL East standings at season's end.

The Angels had won 94 games and the AL West. The Indians had won the Central with the same 96–66 record as the Red Sox—and beat the Yankees in the Division Series. The Angels provided surprisingly little resistance, swept by the Sox by scores of 4–0 (a Josh Beckett shutout), 6–3 (thanks for a three-run walk-off home run by Manny Ramirez), and 9–1 (back-to-back solo home runs in the fourth were enough, but a seven-run seventh sealed the deal).

Beckett beat Cleveland in the first game of the ALCS, but seven runs in the top of the 11th inning at Fenway Park crushed Sox fans hopes to take a 2–0 lead. And the Indians won Games Three and Four, too. Boston was facing elimination, but Beckett held the Tribe to one run in Game Five while his teammates piled up seven runs. The Sox kept rolling, back home in Boston with wins of 12–2 and then 11–2. Manny Ramirez drove in 10 LCS runs and Mike Lowell drove in eight.

The Rockies had an incredible stretch run, winning 14 of their last 15 regular-season games, winning a single-game playoff for the Wild Card slot—and that game took 13 innings. They swept both the NLDS and NLCS. They'd won 21 of 22 games. To say they were on a roll would be an understatement, and they'd even had time to rest up a bit after their back-to-back sweeps, but then…Thump!...they ran into the Red Sox. They were swept. They'd run out of steam.

Beckett went to 4–0 in the postseason with a 13–1 win in Game One. Curt Schilling went to 3–0 with a 2–1 win in Game Two. Daisuke Matsuzaka even drove in two runs of his own on the way to a 10–5 win in Game Three. And the Sox won Game Four, 4–3, Jon Lester getting the win. Mike Lowell was named MVP. For the Red Sox, they had now won back-to-back World Series without losing a game. They were the first team in the twenty-first century to win more than one world championship.

2013—Boston Strong: A Beacon of Bearded Light

Kids born in the year 2000 became teenagers in 2013. They had never known anything of the agony of waiting decades and decades for the Red Sox to win. For them, the Red Sox were world champions over and over again. They had seen some bad Boston baseball, however. As noted, the Red Sox finished in last place in 2012 (with their worst record in nearly 50 years) and both 2014 and 2015. In the middle was 2013, an anomaly?

The team was solid, though. They were 8–4 through a walk-off win on April 15. As they were on their way out of town, a terrorist bomb exploded not far from the finish line of the Boston Marathon, killing three. A couple of days later, a shootout with the terrorists caused the City of Boston and nearby cities to shut down. This was a team of low expectations, but a team that was truly a team. Even in spring training, most had begun to grow bears and they truly became a band of bearded brothers.[1] The

1 See Bill Nowlin and Jim Prime, *From The Babe to the Beards* (New York: Sports Publishing, 2014) for a history of the Red Sox in the World Series from 1903 through 2013.

attack seemed to unite an already strong team under the slogan "Boston Strong." They dipped down to second place a couple of times, but from July 31 on were in first place.

There were no sweeps, but in none of the postseason series did they reach an elimination game, winning with a game to spare in all three rounds—beating the Rays, the Tigers, and the Cardinals. All David Ortiz did in the World Series was to bat .688 (11 for 16), with two doubles and two homers. With eight bases on balls, he had a .760 on-base percentage. Jon Lester was 2-0, allowing just one run over 15 1/3 innings. Fan favorite Koji Uehara had worked in 73 regular-season games with a 1.09 ERA and at one point the Red Sox closer had retired 37 consecutive batters—more than a perfect game. In the postseason, Koji saved seven of the 11 games the Red Sox won—two in the ALDS, three in the ALCS (he also got a win in Game Two), and two in the World Series. And he picked off Kolten Wong with a throw to first base for the final out of Game Four. The game he'd won was the second game of the ALCS, following Big Papi's dramatic grand slam into the Red Sox bullpen in the bottom of the eighth inning. In Game Six, Shane Victorino hit a grand slam of his own in the bottom of the seventh. When they won the World Series at home on October 30, it had been 95 years since the Sox had celebrated winning a World Series in their home ballpark.

2018—The Most Dominant Red Sox Team of All Time?

For four long seasons, Red Sox fans were deprived of world championships. The first two years saw the Sox finish in last place in the AL East, winning only 71 games in 2014 and 78 in 2015. In the next two years, they finished first in the AL East, with 93 wins each year. In 2016, they were swept by Terry Francona's Cleveland Indians in the Division Series and in 2017 they lost three-games-to-one to the ultimate world champion Houston Astros.

In 2018, they put it all together.

In the team's history, they had only won 100 or more regular-season games on three occasions (1912—105, 1915—101, and 1946—104). There were seven times they had lost 100 or more games, and most Red Sox fans—except the youngest ones—were far more accustomed to losing.

In 2018, they won 108 regular-season games.

Even throwing in the postseason wins, the most games any Red Sox team had ever won was in 2004 (98 games in the regular season and the requisite 11 wins in that year's postseason). The total comes to 109 games. In 2018, they won 108 before even getting to the playoffs. And then won 11 more for a grand total of 119. That's a full 10 more wins than in any other year in team history.[2]

The 2018 Red Sox finished eight games ahead of the Yankees in the AL East, then won the ALDS over those same Yankees, three games to one. They beat the reigning world champion Astros in the ALCS, an Astros team that had won 103 regular-season games. They beat the Astros, four games to one. Come to the World Series, once more they only suffered one loss, taking four out of five games from the Dodgers. The Red Sox postseason record was 11–3. They'd won all the games they played, save one game in each round.

Yes, there had been years such as 1967, when the Red Sox had taken the World Series to the decisive Game Seven. Since 2004, their World Series record has been 16–3. It's been a whole different world.

---

2 For a more detailed exploration of the 2018 season—and how it stacks up against the best Yankees team of all time, see Bill Nowlin and David Fischer, *Red Sox vs. Yankees* (New York: Sports Publishing, 2019).

Then came 2019, when they dropped to third place in the AL East—19 games behind the Yankees, and 2020, when they only won 24 games all year long (OK, to be fair, they only played 60 games due to the pandemic, but it was still their second-worst winning percentage since 1930.)

Ups and downs, for sure, but one can still savor the memories of the good times—the championship years.

For most people, that wasn't the case in 1967. There weren't many alive that could hark back to the 1912–1918 era. The 1967 team was light a bolt out of the blue, totally unexpected, a magical year that came out of almost nowhere and transformed a franchise that seemed to be sinking deeper and deeper into a doldrums. That year's team arrived at just the right time for a new generation of fans just a little over 20 years after the Second World War. Socially, politically, culturally, the Sixties were a moment of blossoming in America and the "Impossible Dream Red Sox" had an impact that one could argue still reverberates more than half a century later.

—Bill Nowlin, 2021

EPILOGUE

AFTER 1967

Carl Yastrzemski, to nobody's surprise, was named the American League's Most Valuable Player in 1967. The only surprise was that it wasn't unanimous. One of the two Minnesota writers doing the balloting gave his first-place vote to the Twins' Cesar Tovar. The MVP was just one of the multitude of awards Yaz garnered, including the diamond-studded, solid gold-buckled Hickok Belt (worth $10,000) as the Professional Athlete of the Year and the Sportsman of the Year award from *Sports Illustrated.* Not until Detroit's Miguel Cabrera in 2012 would another player win the Triple Crown.

Jim Lonborg, who finished the regular season with a 22–9 record and a 3.16 ERA and led the AL with 246 strikeouts, won the Cy Young Award as the league's best pitcher. He got 18 of the 20 votes cast. Chicago's Joel Horlen picked up the other two.

Yaz and George Scott both earned Gold Gloves for fielding excellence, and Dick O'Connell was named Major League Executive of the Year by the *Sporting News* and United Press International.

Dick Williams was named Manager of the Year by both major wire services and the *Sporting News,* and influential *New York Times* sports columnist Red Smith wrote the epitaph to the Country Club Era of the Red Sox: "Williams could walk across Boston Harbor daily without stirring wider admiration than he has won by the equally implausible feat of keeping his blithe young spirits in the race and out of the fleshpots."

BREAKING UP THAT OLD GANG OF MINE

I wish I could tell you that our club remained intact, won the pennant and World Series in 1968, and went on to win several more pennants and world championships. We were young enough to have done it. But the only constant in baseball is change.

"People always told me that if you get to the World Series your first or second year, you'll be back many times," George Scott reflected many years after his career ended. "That's not true. I got to the World Series in my second year, and I never got there again."

Neither did Ken Brett, our youngest member of the team at the age of 19 who went on to have a solid major-league career and pitched until 1981. "Being lucky enough to participate in a World Series at my age was unreal," he told longtime Red Sox broadcaster Ken Coleman in 1987. "I only wish I was old enough to really appreciate what I was involved in at such a young age." Ken died of brain cancer in 2003. He was 55.

We thought we would be an even better club in 1968, but we were never really in the race. We played only .500 ball until the Fourth of July, and by then we were 12 games behind the Detroit Tigers, who went on to win the pennant and the World Series. We ended up winning 86 games, only six fewer than in 1967, but finished 17 games out. The magic was gone. It was a grind again. We had to struggle for every hit, struggle for every out.

Of course, we didn't have Tony Conigliaro at all that year. Jim Lonborg broke his leg skiing during the winter and slumped to a 6–10 record with a 4.29 ERA. We thought he'd be all right by the start of the year, but he wasn't, and Lonnie was never a dominating pitcher again. The Red Sox traded him to Milwaukee after the 1971 season, and he later enjoyed a couple of very good years with Philadelphia, winning 17 games in 1974 and 18 in 1976 while helping the Phillies into the playoffs in 1976 and 1977. Lonnie retired in 1979 with a 157–137 record and 3.86 ERA and became a dentist.

Jose Santiago came up with a bad arm in 1968, and although he went 9–4 with a 2.25 ERA, he pitched in only 18 games. The doctors actually stapled the torn tendon to his elbow. (This was about six years before the first successful tendon transplant surgery on pitcher Tommy John.) You could see the little bulge in the skin where the staple was, and you could feel it when you pressed on his arm. Jose's arm never got better, and he pitched only 18 more games in the majors after that.

George Scott, a .303 hitter in 1967, had a nightmarish year in 1968. He hit only .171 with three homers and 25 RBIs in 124 games. He eventually found his stroke again and, after being traded to Milwaukee in the Lonborg deal, had a couple of excellent years for the Brewers. He led the league in homers with 36 and RBIs with 109 in 1975. Boomer was traded back to the Red Sox in 1977 and enjoyed one more productive year with 33 homers and 95 RBIs before retiring two years later. He passed away in 2013.

Mike Andrews, traded to the Chicago White Sox after the 1970 season for Luis Aparicio, got back to the World Series with Dick Williams and the Oakland Athletics in 1973. But his body was pretty well beat up by then, and when he made two errors in the 12th inning that cost Oakland Game 2 of the Series, owner Charlie Finley tried unsuccessfully to force him off the roster. Andrews retired after that season, although he came back a year later to play one more season in Japan.

Joe Foy hit only .225 with 10 homers for us in 1968 and was left exposed in the expansion draft. He was picked by the Kansas City Royals, and by 1971 he was out of the game. He had some problems with drugs and died of a heart attack at the age of 46 in 1989.

Jerry Adair slumped to a .216 average with just three extra-base hits and 12 RBIs in 74 games for us in 1968 and was also let go in the expansion draft to the Royals. He was released in 1970 and died in 1987 at the age of 50.

Dalton Jones got a lot of playing time with us in 1968 and 1969, then was traded to Detroit. He never hit in Tiger Stadium the way he had for us, though, and was dealt to the Texas Rangers early in the 1972 season. He quit after that year.

Outfielder George Thomas stuck around in a utility role for us, until getting released midway through the 1971 season. Minnesota picked him up but released him at the end of the year. Jose Tartabull played a reserve role in 1968, then was sold to Oakland the following year and finished his career with the Athletics in 1970.

As for our catchers, Elston Howard played one more year for us and retired. He died in 1980 at the age of 51. Russ Gibson played two more years with us and then was sold to the San Francisco Giants. He retired in 1972 and died in 2008. Mike Ryan was traded to Philadelphia after the 1967 season and played seven more years for the Phillies.

John Wyatt pitched only eight games for us in 1968 before being sold to the Yankees, who soon passed him on to Detroit. Wyatt didn't get to pitch in the World Series that year but did get another check. Released by the Tigers the following spring, Wyatt pitched briefly for Oakland before getting released again and retiring. He died in 1998.

Gary Bell pitched well again for us in 1968, going 11–11 with a 3.12 ERA. But he wasn't protected and was lost to the Seattle Pilots in the expansion draft. He retired after the 1969 season. Lee Stange pitched 2 ½ more years for us, mostly in relief, before being sold to the White Sox in 1970. He retired after that year.

Billy Rohr didn't make the club in 1968, was sold to Cleveland, and pitched only 17 more games in the majors. Dave Morehead never really licked his arm problems, was drafted by the Royals, and was released at the end of spring training in 1971. Jerry Stephenson also had chronic arm problems and was released in 1969. He pitched briefly for both the Seattle Pilots and

Los Angeles Dodgers before calling it quits in 1970. He passed away in 2010. Gary Waslewski was a reliever and spot starter for us in 1968 and was traded to St. Louis after the season. He bounced around the majors for another four years. Dan Osinski was released at the end of spring training in 1968, latched on with the White Sox, and retired in 1970. He died in 2013. Bill Landis had a very good year for us in 1968 but struggled the following year and was released. Darrell Brandon was hurt most of 1968, went to Seattle in the expansion draft, was injured most of that year, but did come back to pitch in the majors until 1973.

Ken Harrelson had a tremendous year for us in 1968, belting 35 homers and leading the American League in runs batted in with 109. He finished third in the MVP voting and was named the league's Player of the Year by baseball's bible, the *Sporting News*. The Hawk loved Boston, and Boston loved him. But when Tony C. made a successful, albeit temporary, comeback in 1969, the Hawk became expendable. The Red Sox were desperate for pitching and swapped him to the Cleveland Indians early that year for Sonny Siebert, Vicente Romo, and catcher Joe Azcue.

Hawk was devastated by the trade. Cleveland may as well have been Siberia as far as he was concerned. He refused to report to the Indians and threatened to retire and become a professional golfer. The Indians had to renegotiate his contract before the deal went through. Harrelson hit 27 homers, drove in 84 runs, and even stole 17 bases for the Indians in 1969 but was never happy playing in a city where nobody cared about him or baseball. When he broke his ankle sliding into home 17 games into the 1970 season, the injury pretty much ended his baseball career. After playing just 52 more games in 1971, Hawk retired at the age of 29.

Reggie Smith went on to become a seven-time All-Star. He had so much talent, a switch-hitter with great speed and all the tools. He led the league in doubles with 37 in 1968 and blossomed in 1969, hitting .309 with 25 homers and 93 RBIs. He clubbed 30 homers and drove in 96 runs in 1971. But Boston was a tough place for him, and I don't think Reggie ever felt comfortable there. I don't know whether it was because the fans got on him sometimes, or if it might have been a racial thing. While he had some real good years with the Red Sox, it never seemed like he enjoyed the game as much as he should have. He was finally traded to St. Louis after the 1973 season, and he hit .309 with 23 homers and 100 RBIs for the Cardinals in 1974. Reggie was dealt to the Dodgers in 1976 and batted .307 with 32 homers, 104 runs, and 87 RBIs in 1977. He played in three more World Series for the Dodgers before retiring after the 1982 season with a .287 average, 314 homers, and 1,092 RBIs.

Sparky Lyle also went on to enjoy a stellar career. He had a 20-save season for us in 1970 but was traded to the Yankees in a lamentable deal for first baseman Danny Cater a year later, arguably the worst trade of Dick O'Connell's tenure as GM. Lyle played a major role in the revival of the Yankees, leading the AL with 35 saves in 1972 and again with 23 in 1976 when they won their first pennant in 12 years. Lyle won the Cy Young Award in 1977 when he saved 26 games and won 13 others. He pitched in two World Series for the Yankees, going 1–0 with five saves and a 1.23 ERA. Sparky was among the all-time leaders in saves when he retired in 1982.

And then there was Carl Yastrzemski. He was our elder statesman in 1967 and was still going strong years after most of the rest of us had retired. He won his third batting title in 1968—the only man in the AL to hit .300 that year—and put together 40-homer, 100-RBI seasons in 1969 and 1970. But those performances weren't quite good enough for Red Sox fans. After 1967 Yaz, like Ted Williams before him, had set an impossibly high standard for himself to maintain. And, like Williams, Yaz began hearing boos from the fans every time he batted. But he never complained or criticized the fans and stoically continued to play to the best of his abilities.

The fans didn't seem to notice that after '67 teams stopped pitching to Yaz. They'd just walk him because, after Tony C. went down, we never had a real big threat to bat behind him. Tony was a feared hitter, a tough out. Hawk Harrelson hit behind Yaz in '68 and had a great year because he got the pitches to hit that Yaz didn't. As good as Hawk's production was, he still couldn't force teams to pitch to Yaz. After Hawk got traded I batted behind him for a while, and that's why I hit nine grand slams during my career. They'd walk Yaz with a base open and take their chances with me, and I came through a few times. His 1,845 career walks still ranked sixth on the all-time list in 2006.

It wasn't until midway through the 1975 season, when we were finally on our way to winning another pennant, that the fans realized what a treasure they truly had in Yaz, and the booing abruptly stopped. Yaz, by then 36 years old, played like it was '67 all over again when we swept the three-time defending world champion Athletics in the 1975 playoffs. He hit .310 in the World Series against the Cincinnati Reds and had back-to-back 100-RBI seasons in 1976–77 when he was approaching his 40th birthday. He collected his 3,000th hit and 400th homer in 1979 and finished his career in 1983 with a .285 average, 3,419 hits, 452 homers, and 1,844 RBIs. At the age of 44 he could still pull a Nolan Ryan fastball. Yaz was elected to the Hall of Fame in his first year of eligibility in 1989. He was named on 95 percent of the ballots, the seventh-highest percentage in history. The Red Sox retired his No. 8 that same year.

After winning the pennant Dick Williams was rewarded with a three-year contract worth $50,000 a year. He was fired less than two years later on September 23, 1969. We had an 82–71 record and were in third place, but we were 24 games behind the Baltimore Orioles, who ran away with the East Division title (that was the first year each of the two major leagues had been divided into two divisions) and won the pennant.

We could see it coming. Dick tried to remain a disciplinarian. But those of us who were still left from the '67 club were older now and had tasted success, and by the third year of his reign that act was getting old. I think Dick's downfall began in Oakland. Yaz was on third, hesitated coming home on a groundball, and was thrown out. When he got back to the bench, Williams was steaming. "That's going to cost you $500," he told him. Williams thought Yaz wasn't hustling, and he embarrassed him right in front of everybody. After that the resentment just kept building against Dick.

After coaching for a year in Montreal, Williams returned to manage the Oakland Athletics in 1971, leading them to three straight AL West titles, two pennants, and two World Series championships. By then Williams was no longer the gruff, Marine-style drill sergeant with the brush-cut hair we had known in 1967. The Athletics were a free-spirited bunch who defied baseball convention by wearing long hair and mustaches and sometimes brawled with each other in the clubhouse. Williams adopted the mod look of his players. But tired of the meddling by owner Charlie Finley, especially after the embarrassing incident with Mike Andrews during the 1973 World Series, Williams resigned after that season. George Steinbrenner, the new owner of the Yankees who was rebuilding the club, immediately hired him. But Finley protested, telling the Yankees that Williams still had another year on his contract and would either manage the A's or nobody. Steinbrenner had to back off.

Midway through the 1974 season California Angels owner Gene Autry asked Finley for permission to hire Williams, and it was granted. But the Angels never came close to a winning record, and he was fired in the summer of 1976. Williams took over the Montreal Expos, a 1969 expansion team, the following year and led them to two second-place finishes before being fired late in the 1981 season when they were on the verge of making the playoffs for the first and only time in their existence. He took over another rag-tag expansion franchise, the San Diego Padres, the following year and guided them to their first pennant in 1984. He managed yet another expansion franchise, the Seattle Mariners, before being fired in June of 1988 and retiring from managing. In 21 seasons, teams managed by Dick Williams won 1,571 games and lost 1,451 while winning four pennants and two World Series. During that time he also became the first manager to earn a six-figure salary.

A few years later I happened to read Dick's autobiography, *No More Mr. Nice Guy,* in which he related the terrible upbringing he had and all the anger it generated in him. Had I known about that when I was playing for him, I might have thought of him a lot differently and understood him a lot better and why he acted the way he did. We all might have. On the other hand, it probably would not have been the best thing for us as a team if we had known all that in 1967. We might have reacted differently when he barked at us. Instead of getting mad and saying: 'We'll show him!"—which is what we often did—we might have felt sympathy for him and lost our drive. We might have started telling ourselves: "Hey, don't take his tantrums seriously. Dick's really a good guy underneath all that. He just had a tough childhood."

A few years before he passed away in 2011, Dick Williams freely confessed that his managing style would not have worked in the world of modern, corporate baseball. "I got a lot of guys mad," he said on the night he was inducted into the Red Sox Hall of Fame in 2006. "Nowadays you couldn't do that. If I were managing now, I'd probably last a week."

GROWING UP

As for me, 1967 was the year I reached maturity, both as a ballplayer and a person. Until then I constantly worried if I had what it took to be a big-league player.

Having been a hitting star in high school and then watching my batting average decline every time I climbed the ladder in the minors, I began to have a lot of doubts about my ability by the time I reached Triple-A. While I was in Seattle and struggling to hit .230, I kept writing letters to Eddie Popowski, my manager the previous year in Double-A, telling him things like I was thinking about giving up baseball and becoming a drummer or a carpenter. Pop would write me back and say: "I don't know what kind of drummer or carpenter you'd be. But I know you can be a good ballplayer." Pop kept my spirits up and kept me going. But even after I'd reached the majors and stuck with the Red Sox, I worried about being released when I didn't hit, and when I was hitting I was worried about the next slump. If I got released, how could I support my growing family? I couldn't relax. The pressure to succeed, most of it self-imposed, was enormous.

"The Impossible Dream" season changed everything for me. Because of the wrist injury that would not heal, I finished the year batting .259 with 17 homers and 66 RBIs after my terrific start. But it had been a good year for me personally, and instead of fretting about the way I ended it I thought about how much better it could have been if I had been able to swing the bat with more authority. I now knew I had it in me to be better.

That said, I did not have a particularly good year in 1968, batting .234 with 12 homers and 46 RBIs in 123 games. But almost every hitter in baseball had a tough year that summer. It was dubbed "The Year of the Zero" because pitchers dominated and hurled shutouts at the rate of more than two per day, a total of 339 by season's end. No wonder fans were becoming disenchanted with baseball. The game had become a colossal bore. The league batting averages were .243 in the National and .230 in the American, so I actually exceeded the AL average by four points. Yaz won the batting crown with a .301 average, and only five batters in the NL hit over .300. Major League Baseball responded by lowering the height of the mound in 1969 to give the batters a better hitting plane. That helped a little bit. But by 1973 baseball was so desperate for offense, the American League broke with tradition and introduced the designated hitter.

In 1969 I hit .297 and set a record for American League shortstops by clouting 40 homers, breaking the 20-year-old record of 39 set by another Red Sox shortstop, Vern Stephens, back in 1949. (Ernie Banks held the NL record with 47.) I knew I had power, but I never thought of myself as a power hitter until that year. I was 20 pounds heavier by then, and when I hit a ball, it went. I might get under a ball, and it would still carry out of the ballpark. I made the All-Star team again, knocked in 97 runs, drew 98 walks, and scored 92 runs. I finished second to Oakland's Reggie Jackson in slugging percentage with a .589 mark and was fourth in the league in homers, doubles (32), and on-base percentage (.407) and fifth in total bases (315). My home run record stood for nearly 30 years, until Seattle's Alex Rodriguez hit 42 homers in 1998. In the field I set a Red Sox record for shortstops by playing 48 consecutive games without making an error.

I had another real good year in 1970, hitting .261 with 29 homers, 31 doubles, and 103 RBIs. After the Red Sox traded Mike Andrews to the White Sox for Luis Aparicio, a future Hall of Famer, I moved over to third base in 1971 and hit .251 with 28 homers and 89 RBIs while setting a fielding record there by playing 77 straight games without an error. My power began to diminish after that season. I had constant pain in my elbow, the consequence of an injury I had suffered while pitching in high school. The pain had come and gone throughout my career, and now it was there all the time. I took 14 cortisone shots in 1972, but the relief never lasted for more than a day. I found out later that Dr. Tom Tierney, the club physician, had been injecting the cortisone directly into a calcium deposit I had in my elbow. He didn't know it was there. I finally submitted to surgery in 1973. But my good power did not come back, although I continued to drive in runs for the Red Sox.

We came within a whisker of winning the American League East Division title and getting into the playoffs in 1972. A players strike delayed the start of the season by a few days, and the unplayed games were canceled. Because of the uneven schedule, we ended up playing one less game than the Detroit Tigers. They went 86–70, we went 85–70, and we lost the title by a half-game.

By 1975 Yaz and I were the only ones left from the '67 team, except for Tony C., who was trying an unsuccessful comeback that would end in June. But, stocked with young and talented players like Fred Lynn, Jim Rice, Carlton Fisk, Rick Burleson, and Dwight Evans—all of whom had been developed in the Red Sox organization—we won another pennant. I hit a home run in our sweep of the Athletics in the ALCS and hit .308 with four RBIs against the Reds in the World Series.

But my power was completely gone. Still bothered by the dizzy spells after getting beaned by Jim Slaton two years earlier, I became a part-time player in 1976 and hit only .213 with three homers. The Red Sox released me the following spring. I was still only 33, but I'd had a good career, hitting .251 with 210 homers and 773 RBIs in 1,553 games and playing in two World Series. And, of course, there would always be "The Impossible Dream" to cherish. How many players ever get to have a memory like that one?

HOW WE SAVED THE RED SOX

"The Impossible Dream" not only reversed the fortunes of the Red Sox, it saved the franchise. It might even have saved Major League Baseball from becoming an irrelevant sport. It took us eight years to get back to the World Series, and by then fans, increasingly bored with baseball, were deserting the game in many American cities. But it has been written that the pulsating 1975 World Series between the Red Sox and Cincinnati Reds rekindled the passions of the public and resurrected baseball from its deathbed. The game has been thriving and setting attendance records ever since. But what if the Boston Red Sox had ceased to exist before 1975?

It could have happened. Just about the time we were becoming a contender in mid-June of 1967, longtime owner Thomas A. Yawkey dropped a nuclear bomb on Boston. He talked about selling the Red Sox, or moving the franchise to another city, unless Boston or Massachusetts built a modern ballpark for the team. It was front-page news.

Dick O'Connell, the general manager of the Red Sox, had broadly hinted at Mr. Yawkey's mood two weeks earlier in a luncheon speech to members of the newly created BoSox Club at the Hotel Somerset in Boston. We were playing unexpectedly well, and attendance was up 90,000. So no one took O'Connell's comments seriously, and they were buried on the inside pages of the sports sections in the city's newspapers.

"A ball club cannot make money at Fenway Park," O'Connell said. "Finish in the first division and you might break even. Otherwise Tom Yawkey pays the deficit. Yawkey's pocketbook has kept us going. But he's not getting any younger. I know he wants to keep the team here, and his will provides for this. But the time will come when the Red Sox will have to ask whoever runs

Yawkey's estate for some money to pay the annual loss, and that man is gonna say: 'Hey, this is a bad investment. Let's sell it.' And that could be the end of the team here.

"The ballpark is just not built for making money," O'Connell continued. "People say push the left-field fence back and put seats there, but seats in the outfield don't sell in advance. We have 8,000 box seats at three dollars. The Yankees have 16,000 at three-fifty. We have bleacher seats at a dollar. Nobody is going to get rich on those."

Fenway Park was 55 years old in 1967, and demographics had changed. Boston's population was shrinking. More and more people were living in the suburbs, and fewer and fewer fans were taking public transportation or walking to games anymore. Fans had to drive, and parking around Fenway was virtually nonexistent. Mr. Yawkey had been asking politely for a new park for more than 10 years, and in that time a half-dozen other major-league cities had built new facilities for their teams. All the politicians in Massachusetts ever did was talk about it. He was 64 years old and running out of patience.

Two weeks after O'Connell's largely ignored speech, the publicity-shy owner finally spoke out in an interview with Will McDonough of the *Boston Globe*.

"This is not a threat; this is a mere statement of fact," Mr. Yawkey began. "I cannot continue indefinitely under present circumstances. I am losing money with the Red Sox and no one—unless he's a damn fool—likes to lose money. Maybe there are people who feel I would wait forever. They probably figure: 'What the hell, that guy has all kinds of money.' But things change, and you can only live with a bad situation for so long. I have come to that realization, and I hope Boston does before it's too late. There was a lot of talk about the Braves leaving before it ever took place, but no one paid any attention. Then, suddenly, they were gone."

Mr. Yawkey indicated he was losing in excess of a million dollars a year, and those were losses even his substantial fortune could not sustain forever. He pointed out that he had purchased the San Francisco Seals of the minor Pacific Coast League in 1956 not just for the purpose of protecting that territory for the American League in the event of expansion but as a potential future home for the Red Sox. He had surrendered that option two years later when the New York Giants moved to San Francisco while the Brooklyn Dodgers relocated to Los Angeles. He didn't say where he was thinking of relocating the Red Sox now, but Milwaukee was certainly a strong possibility. Milwaukee had lured the Braves from Boston in 1953 but had just lost the team to Atlanta and was seeking another club.

"They better not call my bluff," Mr. Yawkey warned the politicians. "I don't bluff. All I have to do is open the door."

His comments spurred a great deal of activity among the politicians, and for the next few weeks all sorts of ballpark proposals were being touted. By late summer a sketch of a proposed $60-million stadium even appeared in the papers. But as the Red Sox kept winning and drawing record crowds, Mr. Yawkey calmed down, and, of course, a new ballpark was never built.

During the interview he was asked if he could envision the Red Sox still playing in Fenway Park five years hence. He said he could not. Fifty years later and more than 40 years after Mr. Yawkey's death, the Red Sox were still playing in Fenway and attracting record crowds. The Red Sox have never been more popular or more profitable. From 2003-13 they sold out a major-league record 820 consecutive home games. In the last years that the Yawkey Estate owned the club, there was serious talk about building a $500-million ballpark adjacent to Fenway, and plans were drawn up and heavily publicized. The project was delayed as traditionalist

Red Sox fans argued against a new and modern park and a downturn in the economy prompted the state to back out of its commitment to share the cost. When the club was sold in 2002 to the John Henry-Tom Werner Group for a record $700 million—more than twice the amount any major-league franchise had ever fetched before—the project was scuttled. Instead the new owners have invested tens of millions of dollars to enlarge and renovate venerable old Fenway Park, and Red Sox fans have never been happier.

"We drew almost a million more fans in '67 than we had the year before, and it just kept getting better and better after that," Dick Williams said in retrospect four decades after winning the pennant. "I'm extremely proud that what we accomplished in '67 turned the Red Sox franchise around. What's happened since then is phenomenal."

Attendance soared from 811,172 in 1966 to a record 1,727,832 in 1967. Except for 1981, when a seven-week players' strike wiped out one-third of the schedule, the Red Sox have never drawn less than 1.44 million. They cracked the two-million mark in 1977 for the first time, and beginning in 1986 they have drawn at least 2.1 million fans to the major leagues' smallest ballpark every season with the exception of 1994, when another strike canceled nearly a third of the schedule.

The 50 years since "The Impossible Dream" have been the longest period of sustained success in Red Sox history with 40 winning seasons and 15 post-season appearances, including five pennants and three World Series titles. The Red Sox had 16 consecutive winning seasons from 1967–82 and only six losing records in those 40 years.

A FINAL LOOK BACK

I think back to that wild and crazy night when we landed at Logan Airport after having won 10 games in a row and were mobbed by

15,000 fans who were so thrilled that the Red Sox were finally in a pennant race they could not contain their emotions. Those little children perched on the shoulders of their dads became the next generation of rabid Red Sox fans.

The memories you have as a kid, the heroes you worshipped, are indelible and stick with you your whole life. No era—whatever era it was you grew up in—will ever be the same or anywhere near as good as that one. The kids who were growing up in 1967 don't feel quite the same about the Red Sox now, even the 2004 team that finally won it all. Sure, they're glad that the Red Sox finally won a World Series after waiting for 86 years. But if you were a kid growing up in 1946, 1967, 1975, 1978, or 1986, you must admit to yourself you would have appreciated that title just a little bit more if the Red Sox team you devoted yourself to heart and soul back then had done it. Wherever I go I always hear the lament: "Baseball has changed. It's not like when you guys played." And the fans of the 2004 World Champion Red Sox will be saying the same thing 20 years from now, even if the Red Sox win five more World Series in that time. Every generation does it. There's something about those childhood memories that can never be topped.

Dave Roberts understands. A journeyman outfielder who has played with six different organizations, Roberts was with the Red Sox for only a few weeks in 2004. But his clutch stolen base—the modern equivalent of Jim Lonborg's bunt in 1967—off the Yankees' Mariano Rivera in Game 4 of the American League Championship Series to set himself up to score the tying run when the Red Sox were three outs away from elimination, igniting an improbable eight-game postseason winning streak that culminated in a World Series title, was enshrined in the Red Sox Hall of Fame as a Memorable Moment two years later. During the induction ceremonies, Roberts talked about how moved he was by the fans during his brief stay with the Red Sox.

"The baseball demographic is older men," he said. "But in Boston, kids grow up listening to their fathers and their grandfathers talking about the Red Sox, and there is no other team in baseball that is like that."

We didn't win the World Series in 1967. But I'm proud of everything we did and accomplished that year, and prouder still that we revived the interest and passion of the fans, created a whole new generation of fans, and restored respectability to the Red Sox franchise.

It wasn't just a dream.